Buttercream Frosting, Cakes & Cupcakes

A Collection of

The Best Recipes

MARIA SOBININA

BRILLIANTkitchenideas.com

DEDICATION

This book is dedicated to my beautiful family and friends, as well as to you, my reader. I am happy to share the amazing joy of preparing healthy meals with you.

MARIA XOXO

TABLE OF CONTENTS

Recipes: Buttercream

American Buttercream

INGREDIENTS:

8 Oz **Butter**, unsalted, softened

2 cups **Sugar**, powdered, sifted

2 tablespoons **Milk**

2 teaspoons **Vanilla**, pure, extract

EQUIPMENT:

Stand or hand mixer fitted with the paddle attachment, Sifter, Food scale or measuring cups set, Cake decorating piping tips and bags (optional).

PREPARATION:

Step 1: Place butter on a kitchen countertop and leave it until it reaches room temperature.

Step 2: In a bowl of stand mixer, fitted with the paddle attachment, beat butter on medium speed, for 2-3 minutes until it becomes soft and light.

Step 3: Gradually add one half of powdered sugar and beat the mixture starting on low speed and continuing on low-medium speed until fully incorporated.

Add vanilla extract. Beat again for 30 seconds.

Slowly add remaining sugar and beat on medium speed until all is fully incorporated and buttercream becomes light and fluffy. Do not overbeat.

Place into the fridge to cool.

Store American Buttercream the refrigerator for up to one week. Beat it with a mixer before using.

Swiss Meringue Buttercream

INGREDIENTS:

12 Oz **Butter**, unsalted, softened

1 cup **Sugar**, powdered, sifted

5 **Egg whites**

1 teaspoon **Vanilla**, pure, extract

¼ teaspoon **Salt**

EQUIPMENT:

Stand or hand mixer fitted with the whisk attachment, Sifter, Heatproof bowl, Food scale or measuring cups set, Cake decorating piping tips and bags (optional).

PREPARATION:

Step 1: Place butter on a kitchen countertop and leave it until it reaches room temperature.

Step 2: Place a heatproof bowl over slowly boiling water bath on low heat. Add egg whites and sugar into the bowl and stir until sugar fully dissolves.

Step 3: Transfer the mixture into a bowl of stand mixer, fitted with the whisk attachment. Beat on medium speed, for 4-5 minutes until meringue becomes thick and glossy.

Step 4: Add softened butter, salt, and vanilla. Beat on medium speed until buttercream becomes silky and smooth.

Place into the fridge to cool.

Store Swiss Meringue Buttercream in the refrigerator for up to one week. Beat it with a mixer before using.

German Buttercream

This buttercream is great as a topping or as a filing. It can be piped to decorate cakes and cupcakes as well.

INGREDIENTS:

8 Oz **Butter**, unsalted, softened

1 cup **Sugar**, cane, granulated

3 **Egg yolks**, large, room temperature

¾ cup **Milk**, whole

1 tablespoon **Cornstarch,** organic (*or Corn four*)

1 teaspoon **Vanilla**, pure, extract

¼ teaspoon **Salt**

EQUIPMENT:

Stand or hand mixer fitted with the paddle attachment, Saucepan, Food scale or measuring cups set, Plastic wrap, Cake decorating piping tips and bags (optional).

PREPARATION:

Step 1: Place butter on a kitchen countertop and leave it until it reaches room temperature.

Step 2: In a bowl of stand mixer, fitted with the

paddle attachment, combine half of the granulated sugar, egg yolks, cornstarch, vanilla extract, and salt. Beat it until it becomes a bit foamy. Set it aside.

Step 3: In a saucepan, combine milk and second half of granulated sugar. Heat the mixture over medium-low heat, constantly stirring. Bring it to simmer, and remove from heat.

Step 4: Add half of the hot milk mixture into egg yolk mixture. Beat with a whisk attachment on low speed. Add the remaining hot milk, little by little.

Step 5: Pour this mixture back into the saucepan, over medium-low heat. Stir constantly with a spatula, until the mixture becomes a thick custard. Remove from heat once the mixture starts bubbling.

Step 6: Cover it with plastic wrap and place into the fridge to cool, for approximately two hours.

Step 7: In a bowl of stand mixer, fitted with the paddle attachment, beat butter on medium speed, for 5-7 minutes until it becomes soft and light.

Step 8: Add cooled custard mixture and beat on high speed with a paddle attachment until it becomes creamy and smooth.

Step 9: Add remaining powdered sugar and then

add half of the key lime juice and half of milk and process mixture until smooth.

For the best results, use immediately.

Store German Buttercream in the refrigerator for up to one week. Beat it with a mixer before using.

Vanilla Cream Buttercream

INGREDIENTS:

8 Oz **Butter**, unsalted, softened

4 cups **Sugar**, powdered, sifted

½ cup **Heavy cream**

2 teaspoons **Vanilla**, pure, extract

Pinch of **Salt**

EQUIPMENT:

Stand or hand mixer fitted with the paddle attachment, Sifter, Food scale or measuring cups set, Cake decorating piping tips and bags (optional).

PREPARATION:

Step 1: Place butter on a kitchen countertop and leave it until it reaches room temperature.

Step 2: In a bowl of stand mixer, fitted with the paddle attachment, beat butter on medium speed, for 3-4 minutes until it becomes soft and light.

Step 3: Gradually add one half of powdered sugar and beat starting on low speed and continuing on low-medium speed until fully incorporated.

Add vanilla extract. Beat again for 30 seconds.

Slowly add remaining sugar and beat on medium speed until all is fully incorporated and buttercream becomes light and fluffy. Do not overbeat.

Step 4: Add heavy cream and beat until it reaches desired consistency. Do not overbeat or buttercream will clump.

Place into the fridge to cool.

Store Vanilla Cream Buttercream in the refrigerator for up to one week. Beat it with a mixer before using.

French Buttercream

INGREDIENTS:

16 oz **Butter**, unsalted, softened

8 **Egg yolks**, large, pasteurized

1 cup **Sugar**, cane, granulated

6 tablespoons **Water**

1 teaspoon **Vanilla**, pure, extract

Pinch of **Salt**

EQUIPMENT:

Stand or hand mixer fitted with the paddle attachment, Medium saucepan, Sifter, Food scale or measuring cups set, Cake decorating piping tips and bags (optional).

PREPARATION:

Step 1: Pasteurize egg yolks over the water bath by bringing water to 140°F and simmering for about three minutes. Set aside to cool.

Step 2: Place cooled egg yolks into a bowl of a stand mixer equipped with a whisk attachment. Beat until it becomes thick and foamy.

Step 3: Combine water and sugar in a medium

saucepan. Heat over low-medium heat until sugar dissolves. Once sugar dissolves increase the heat and bring it to boil. Cook the mixture until it reaches 235°F.

Step 4: Start adding hot syrup into the mixing bowl, continuing mixing on low speed. Mix for 5-7 minutes until syrup cools down.

Step 5: Add butter, one tablespoon at a time, into mixing bowl with the cooled mixture. Continue mixing on low speed until butter incorporates and looks creamy.

Add salt and vanilla and mix again for another 1-2 minutes until all is incorporated and becomes smooth and fluffy.

Place in the fridge to cool.

Store French Buttercream in the refrigerator for up to one week. Beat it with a mixer before using.

Italian Meringue Buttercream

This beautiful buttercream can withstand hot temperatures. This buttercream is perfect to stack tiered cakes (such as wedding cakes).

INGREDIENTS:

1 ¼ cups **Sugar**, cane, granulated

2/3 cup **Maple syrup**

2/3 cup **Water**

5 **Egg whites**

1 1/3 cups **Butter,** unsalted, softened

2 2/3 cups **Shortening**, vegetable

2 teaspoons **Vanilla**, pure, extract

EQUIPMENT:

Stand or hand mixer fitted with the paddle attachment, Medium heat-proof bowl, Candy thermometer, Cake decorating piping tips and bags (optional).

PREPARATION:

Step 1: In a heat-proof medium bowl combine sugar, maple syrup, and water. Bring to a boil over medium-high heat. Constantly stir the mixture and heat it to 223°F to 234°F.

The mixture is ready when it forms a soft thread when it is dripped from a spatula. This should take 1 or 2 minutes. Once it is ready, remove it from heat and set aside.

Step 2: Add egg whites into a bowl of stand mixer fitted with the paddle attachment. Beat on low and then on medium speed until it can hold a stiff peak.

Slowly pour sugar syrup mixture in a thin stream, while continuing to whip at a medium speed. Continue mixing for another 10 minutes. Set aside.

Step 3: Add pieces of cold butter one at a time. Continue to beat at medium speed until butter incorporates into the mixture.

Step 4: Add vegetable shortening and continue mixing at a medium speed.

The buttercream will break down and look crumbled. Keep mixing for another 10 minutes until it will become smooth and glossy.

Place into the fridge to cool.

Store Italian Meringue Buttercream in the refrigerator for up to one week. Beat it with a mixer before using.

This recipe contains raw egg. We recommend that pregnant women, young children, the elderly, and the infirm do not consume raw egg.

Buttercream for Flower Piping

INGREDIENTS:

16 Oz **Butter**, unsalted, softened

4 cups **Sugar**, powdered, sifted

¼ cup **Corn flour**, organic *(or Corn starch)*

¼ cup **Cream,** heavy, whipping

2 teaspoons **Vanilla**, pure, extract

1 teaspoon **Salt,** sea

EQUIPMENT:

Stand or hand mixer fitted with the paddle attachment, Sifter, Food scale or measuring cups set, Cake decorating piping tips and bags (optional).

PREPARATION:

Step 1: Place butter and all other ingredients on a kitchen countertop and leave it until it reaches room temperature.

Step 2: In a bowl of stand mixer, fitted with the paddle attachment, beat butter on medium speed, for 2-3 minutes until it becomes soft and light.

Step 3: Add heavy cream, corn flour, and salt. Mix

until all is incorporated to remove any lumps. You may add a bit of powdered sugar to aid the mixing process. Check that all is mixed evenly scraping the bottom of the mixing bowl.

Step 4: Gradually add one-third of powdered sugar and beat starting on low speed and continuing on medium speed until fully incorporated.

Add vanilla extract. Beat again for thirty seconds to one minute.

Slowly add remaining sugar and beat on medium speed until all is fully incorporated and buttercream becomes light and fluffy. Scrape the sides of the bowl and mix again.

Place into the fridge to cool.

Store Buttercream for Flower Piping in the refrigerator for up to one month (or up to 6 months in a freezer). Beat it with a mixer before using.

Notes: if the buttercream is too stiff, add more heavy cream. If it is too liquid, add more powdered sugar. (Both – teaspoon at a time).

Cream Cheese Buttercream

INGREDIENTS:

8 Oz **Butter**, unsalted, softened

8 Oz **Cream cheese,** softened

2 cups **Sugar**, powdered, sifted

1 teaspoon **Vanilla**, pure, extract

EQUIPMENT:

Stand or hand mixer fitted with the paddle attachment, Sifter, Food scale or measuring cups set, Cake decorating piping tips and bags (optional).

PREPARATION:

Step 1: Place butter and cream cheese on a kitchen countertop and leave it until it reaches room temperature.

Step 2: In a bowl of stand mixer, fitted with the paddle attachment, beat cream cheese on medium speed, for 4-5 minutes until it achieved a smooth consistency.

Step 3: Add softened butter, (one quester at a time) and beat on medium speed, for another 5-7 minutes until mixture becomes soft and light.

Step 4: Gradually add one half of powdered sugar and beat starting on low speed and continuing on medium speed until fully incorporated. Add vanilla extract and beat for another 30 seconds to one minute.

Step 5: Add remaining powdered sugar and beat until all is incorporated and buttercream becomes smooth and fluffy.

Place into the fridge to cool.

Store Cream Cheese Buttercream in the refrigerator for up to one week. Beat it with a mixer before using.

Quick and Simple Buttercream

This is a great "base" buttercream.

INGREDIENTS:

4 Oz **Butter**, unsalted, softened

2 cups **Sugar**, cane, powdered

2 tablespoons Milk, whole

1 teaspoon **Vanilla**, pure, extract

1 teaspoon **Almond**, pure, extract

EQUIPMENT:

Stand or hand mixer fitted with the paddle attachment, Cake decorating piping tips and bags (optional).

PREPARATION:

Step 1: Place butter on a kitchen countertop and leave it until it reaches room temperature.

Step 2: In a bowl of stand mixer, fitted with the paddle attachment, add butter and beat it at medium speed until it becomes smooth and fluffy.

Step 3: Gradually add powdered sugar and beat until it is fully incorporated. Add vanilla extract and beat for another 30 seconds.

Step 4: Add milk and beat for another 45 seconds. Do not overbeat.

Place into the fridge to cool.

Store Quick and Simple Buttercream in the refrigerator for up to one week. Beat it with a mixer before using.

Banana Buttercream

This buttercream is light and fluffy. It is great for chocolate cakes and cupcakes.

INGREDIENTS:

8 Oz **Whipped topping**, frozen, thawed

3.5 Oz **Banana pudding**, instant, mix

1 **Banana**, very ripe, mashed

1 cup **Milk**

2 tablespoons **Rum**

EQUIPMENT:

Stand or hand mixer fitted with the paddle attachment, Cake decorating piping tips and bags (optional).

PREPARATION:

Step 1: In a bowl of stand mixer, fitted with the paddle attachment, combine banana pudding, mashed banana, milk, and rum.

Beat on a low to medium speed until mixture becomes very thick.

Step 2: Gently beat in thawed whipped topping. Continue to beat until it becomes smooth.

Place into the fridge to cool.

Store Banana Buttercream in the refrigerator for up to one week. Beat it with a mixer before using.

Hazelnut Buttercream

This frosting is wonderful for chocolate cakes.

INGREDIENTS:

8 Oz **Cream cheese**, softened

4 Oz cup **Butter**, unsalted, softened

1 cup **Chocolate-hazelnut**, spread

1 tablespoon **Milk**

EQUIPMENT:

Stand or hand mixer fitted with the paddle attachment, Cake decorating piping tips and bags (optional).

PREPARATION:

Step 1: Place butter and cream cheese on a kitchen countertop and leave it until it reaches room temperature.

Step 2: In a bowl of stand mixer, fitted with the paddle attachment, beat cream cheese on medium speed, for 4-5 minutes until it becomes soft and fluffy.

Step 3: Little by little add softened butter and beat on medium speed until all is incorporated and fluffy.

Step 4: Add hazelnut spread and milk and continue beating until smooth and fluffy.

Place into the fridge to cool.

Store Hazelnut Buttercream in the refrigerator for up to one week. Beat it with a mixer before using.

Lemon Cream Cheese Buttercream

This Lemon Cream Cheese Buttercream is perfect for lemon drops.

INGREDIENTS:

4 Oz **Cream cheese**, softened

4 Oz **Butter**, unsalted, softened

2 ¼ cups **Sugar**, cane, powdered *and*

1 cup **Sugar**, cane, powdered

2 tablespoons **Lemon juice**

EQUIPMENT:

Stand or hand mixer fitted with the paddle attachment, Medium mixing bowl, Cake decorating piping tips and bags (optional).

PREPARATION:

Step 1: Place butter and cream cheese on a kitchen countertop and leave it until it reaches room temperature.

Step 2: In a bowl of stand mixer, fitted with the paddle attachment, add cream cheese and beat it at medium speed until it becomes smooth.

Little by little, add softened butter and continue mixing until it becomes smooth and fluffy.

Step 3: Add one cup of powdered sugar and lemon juice and beat for 30 seconds.

Step 4: Little by little, add the remaining 2 ¼ cups of powdered sugar. Beat until buttercream becomes creamy and light.

Place into the fridge to cool.

Store Lemon Cream Buttercream in the refrigerator for up to one week. Beat it with a mixer before using.

Raspberry Buttercream

Perfect buttercream for any cake that calls for a fruity flavor.

INGREDIENTS:

FOR THE BUTTERCREAM:

2 cups **Sugar**, powdered

1 cup **Butter**, unsalted, softened

1 teaspoon **Vanilla**, pure, extract

For the Raspberry Puree:

1 cup **Raspberries**, fresh or frozen, thawed

2 tablespoons **Cream,** heavy, whipping

EQUIPMENT:

Stand or hand mixer fitted with the paddle attachment, Cake decorating piping tips and bags (optional).

PREPARATION:

MAKE THE PUREE:

Step 1: In a blender, puree raspberries and heavy cream until smooth.

Transfer into a small saucepan, add two tablespoons of powdered sugar and reduce the liquid by simmering over low heat. Set aside to cool.

MAKE THE BUTTERCREAM:

Step 1: Place butter and on a kitchen countertop and leave it until it reaches room temperature.

Step 2: In a bowl of stand mixer, fitted with the paddle attachment, beat butter on medium speed, for 3-4 minutes until it becomes soft and light.

Step 3: Gradually add powdered sugar and beat until fully incorporated. Add vanilla extract and beat again for 30 seconds.

Step 4: Add raspberries puree and beat for another 45 seconds. Do not overbeat.

Place into the fridge to cool.

Store Raspberry Buttercream in the refrigerator for up to one week. Beat it with a mixer before using.

Black Volcano Buttercream

Great buttercream icing for chocolate or caramel cakes.

INGREDIENTS:

12 Oz **Condensed milk**, sweetened

8 Oz **Butter**, unsalted, softened

2 cups **Sugar**, powdered

1/2 cup **Cocoa powder**, Dutch, unsweetened

1 teaspoon **Vanilla**, pure, extract

EQUIPMENT:

Stand or hand mixer fitted with the paddle attachment, Cake decorating piping tips and bags (optional).

PREPARATION:

Step 1: Place butter and on a kitchen countertop and leave it until it reaches room temperature.

Step 2: In a bowl of stand mixer, fitted with the paddle attachment, beat butter on medium speed, for 3-4 minutes until it becomes soft and light.

Step 3: Gradually add powdered sugar and beat until fully incorporated. Add vanilla extract and beat again for 30 seconds.

Step 4: Add condensed milk and cocoa powder and beat until smooth. Do not overbeat.

Place into the fridge to cool.

Store Black Volcano Buttercream in the refrigerator for up to one week. Beat it with a mixer before using.

White Chocolate Buttercream

INGREDIENTS:

8 Oz **Butter**, unsalted, softened

8 Oz **Chocolate**, white, bakers

1 teaspoon **Vanilla**, pure, extract

EQUIPMENT:

Stand or hand mixer fitted with the paddle attachment, Food scale or measuring cups set, Medium saucepan, Cake decorating piping tips and bags (optional).

PREPARATION:

Step 1: Combine butter and white chocolate in a medium saucepan. Place it over low heat constantly stirring the mixture. When butter and chocolate are fully melted remove saucepan from heat.

Step 2: Set aside the mixture in room temperature for 20-30 minutes. When the mixture cools off to room temperature, place saucepan into the fridge and refrigerate for about three hours.

Step 3: After three hours, remove frosting from the fridge and let it sit at room temperature for 30 to 45 minutes.

Step 4: Transfer the buttercream into a bowl of stand mixer, fitted with the paddle attachment. Add vanilla extract. Beat the mixture on medium speed, for 5-7 minutes until it becomes soft and light.

Place into the fridge to cool.

Store White Chocolate Buttercream in the refrigerator for up to one week. Beat it with a mixer before using.

Strawberry Cream Cheese Frosting

Good buttercream for many kinds of cakes, including, chocolate or white cakes.

INGREDIENTS:

4 Oz **Cream cheese**, softened

4 Oz **Butter**, unsalted, softened

1 1/4 cups **Sugar**, powdered

1/2 cup **Cream**, heavy whipping

1/4 cup **Strawberry**, puree

1/2 teaspoon **Vanilla**, pure extract

EQUIPMENT:

Stand or hand mixer fitted with the paddle attachment, Cake decorating piping tips and bags (optional).

PREPARATION:

Step 1: Place butter and cream cheese on a kitchen countertop and leave it until it reaches room temperature.

Step 2: Chill a large glass or metal bowl and the beaters for 30 minutes.

Step 3: In a large chilled bowl of a stand mixer, beat heavy whipping cream on medium speed, for 5-6 minutes, until stiff peaks start to form.

Step 4: In a separate bowl, beat cream cheese, for 1-2 minutes, until creamy.

Step 5: Add softened butter and continue beating on medium speed, for 3-4 minutes, until it becomes well blended and smooth.

Step 6: Add strawberry puree and vanilla extract. Beat for another 2-3 minutes. Add powdered sugar and beat for 4-5 minutes until it is soft and fluffy.

Step 7: Fold in the whipped cream into the cream cheese mixture until whipped cream is evenly incorporated.

Place into the fridge to cool.

Store Strawberry Cream Cheese Frosting in the refrigerator for up to 1 week. Beat it with a mixer before using.

Dark Chocolate Buttercream

INGREDIENTS:

8 Oz **Butter,** unsalted, softened

8 Oz **Chocolate,** dark, bakers

1 teaspoon **Vanilla,** pure, extract

EQUIPMENT:

Stand or hand mixer fitted with the paddle attachment, Food scale or measuring cups set, Medium saucepan, Cake decorating piping tips and bags (optional).

PREPARATION:

Step 1: Combine butter and dark chocolate in a medium saucepan. Place it over low heat constantly stirring the mixture. When butter and chocolate are fully melted remove saucepan from the heat.

Step 2: Set aside for 20-30 minutes in room temperature. When the mixture cools off, place saucepan into the fridge and refrigerate for about three hours.

Step 3: After three hours, remove frosting from the fridge and let it sit at room temperature for 30 to 45 minutes.

Step 4: Transfer into a bowl of stand mixer, fitted with the paddle attachment. Add vanilla extract. Beat the chocolate mixture on medium speed, for 5-7 minutes until it becomes soft and light.

Place into the fridge to cool.

Store Dark Chocolate Buttercream in the refrigerator for up to one week. Beat it with a mixer before using.

White Chocolate Glaze

INGREDIENTS:

6 Oz **Chocolate**, white, bakers

¼ cup **Heavy,** cream

1 teaspoon **Vanilla**, pure, extract

EQUIPMENT:

Hand whisk, Food scale or measuring cups set, Medium heatproof bowl, Medium saucepan, Cake decorating piping tips and bags (optional).

PREPARATION:

Step 1: Place finely chopped white chocolate into a small heatproof bowl. Set over a warm water bath on low heat. Stir until chocolate melts.

Remove from the heat and stir until smooth.

Step 2: In a small saucepan, heat heavy cream over low heat, constantly stirring until it starts simmering.

Remove from heat. Add 2/3 of hot heavy cream into the bowl with melted white chocolate.

Gently mix it to incorporate gradually adding

remaining heavy cream.

Step 3: Beat with a whisk until smooth.

Place into the fridge to cool.

Store in the refrigerator for up to 1 week. Beat it with a mixer before using.

Caramel Buttercream

INGREDIENTS:

4 Oz **Butter**, unsalted, softened

1 ½ cups **Sugar**, powdered, sifted

1 cup **Sugar**, brown

¼ cup **Cream,** heavy

1 teaspoon **Vanilla**, pure, extract

¼ teaspoon **Salt**

EQUIPMENT:

Stand or hand mixer fitted with the paddle attachment, Medium size saucepan, Sifter, Food scale or measuring cups set, Cake decorating piping tips and bags (optional).

PREPARATION:

Step 1: Melt butter in a saucepan over low heat. Add brown sugar and heavy cream. Cook the mixture, stirring, until the mixture starts bubbling and smells like caramel.

Remove from heat. Add vanilla extract and salt. Let it cool for a few minutes.

Step 2: Transfer caramel into a bowl of stand mixer. Add 1/4 of powdered sugar. Beat the mixture on low speed until all is fully incorporated, then increase speed to medium.

Add vanilla extract and salt. Beat for another 1-2 minutes.

Step 3: Little by little, keep adding the rest of powdered sugar and beat until all is incorporated and the mixture is smooth and light.

Place into the fridge to cool.

Store Caramel Buttercream in the refrigerator for up to one week. Beat it with a mixer before using.

Blueberry Buttercream

INGREDIENTS:

FOR THE BUTTERCREAM:

8 Oz **Butter**, unsalted, softened

2 cups **Sugar**, powdered, sifted

1 teaspoon **Vanilla**, pure, extract

FOR THE BLUEBERRIES PUREE:

1 cup **Blueberries**, frozen, thawed

2 tablespoons **Milk,** whole

EQUIPMENT:

Stand or hand mixer fitted with a paddle attachment, Blender or food processor, Small saucepan, Food scale or measuring cups set, Sifter, Cake decorating piping tips and bags (optional).

PREPARATION:

MAKE THE PUREE:

Step 1: In a blender, puree blueberries and heavy cream until smooth.

Transfer into a small saucepan, add two tablespoons of powdered sugar and reduce the liquid by simmering over low heat. Set aside to cool.

MAKE THE BUTTERCREAM:

Step 1: Place butter on a kitchen countertop and leave it until it reaches room temperature.

Step 2: In a blender, puree blueberries and milk until smooth. Transfer into a small saucepan, add two tablespoons of powdered sugar and reduce the liquid by simmering over low heat. Set aside to cool.

Step 3: In a bowl of stand mixer, fitted with the paddle attachment, beat butter on medium speed, for 3-4 minutes until it becomes soft and light.

Step 4: Gradually add one half of powdered sugar and beat starting on low speed and continuing on medium speed until fully incorporated. Add vanilla extract and beat again for another 30 seconds.

Step 5: Add blueberries puree and beat on medium speed until fully incorporated.

Step 6: Add remaining powdered sugar and beat the mixture until smooth.

Place into the fridge to cool.

Store Blueberry Buttercream in the refrigerator for up to one week. Beat it with a mixer before using.

Dark Horse Chocolate Cream Cheese Buttercream

Amazing buttercream for chocolate cake.

INGREDIENTS:

16 Oz **Cream cheese**, softened

8 Oz **Butter**, unsalted, softened

2 cups **Sugar**, powdered

1/2 cup **Cocoa powder**, Dutch, unsweetened

1 teaspoon **Vanilla**, pure, extract

EQUIPMENT:

Stand or hand mixer fitted with the paddle attachment, Medium mixing bowl, Cake decorating piping tips and bags (optional).

PREPARATION:

Step 1: Place butter and cream cheese on a kitchen countertop and leave it until it reaches room temperature.

Step 2: In a medium mixing bowl combine powdered sugar and Dutch cocoa powder. Set aside.

Step 3: In a bowl of stand mixer, fitted with the paddle attachment, add cream cheese and beat it at a medium speed until mixture becomes smooth.

Little by little, add softened butter and continue mixing until it becomes smooth and fluffy.

Step 4: Add vanilla extract; gradually add powdered sugar and cocoa powder mix, constantly beating on medium speed until all is fully incorporated and buttercream becomes light and fluffy.

Place into the fridge to cool.

Store Dark Chocolate Cream Cheese Buttercream in the refrigerator for up to one week. Beat it with a mixer before using.

Banana Caramel Buttercream

INGREDIENTS:

4 Oz **Butter**, unsalted, softened

1 ½ cups **Sugar**, powdered, sifted

1 cup **Sugar**, brown

1 Banana, **ripe**

¼ cup **Heavy cream**

1 teaspoon **Vanilla**, pure, extract

¼ teaspoon **Salt**

EQUIPMENT:

Stand or hand mixer fitted with the paddle attachment, Medium size saucepan, Sifter, Food scale or measuring cups set, Cake decorating piping tips and bags (optional).

PREPARATION:

Step 1: In a food processor, puree banana until creamy consistency. Set aside.

Step 2: In a saucepan, melt butter over low heat. Add brown sugar and heavy cream.

Cook the mixture stirring, until the mixture starts

bubbling and smells like caramel.

Remove from heat, add vanilla extract, and salt. Let it cool for a few minutes.

Step 3: Transfer caramel into a bowl of stand mixer, add one-quarter of powdered sugar. Beat on low speed until all is incorporated, then increase speed to medium.

Add vanilla extract and salt. Beat for another 30 seconds.

Step 4: Add banana puree and process until all is incorporated.

Step 5: Little by little, keep adding the rest of powdered sugar and beat until all is incorporated and the mixture is smooth and light.

Place into the fridge to cool.

Store Banana Caramel Buttercream in the refrigerator for up to 1 week. Beat it with a mixer before using.

Pineapple Coconut Buttercream

INGREDIENTS:

4 Oz **Butter**, unsalted, softened

4 cups **Sugar**, powdered, sifted

½ cup **Coconut**, shredded, unsweetened

1 tablespoon **Pineapples**, well drained, crushed

1 tablespoon **Pineapples**, juice of

1 teaspoon **Key Lime**, juice of

EQUIPMENT:

Stand or hand mixer fitted with the paddle attachment, Food processor, Sifter, Mesh sieve, Food scale or measuring cups set, Cake decorating piping tips and bags (optional).

PREPARATION:

Step 1: Place butter on a kitchen countertop and leave it until it reaches room temperature.

Step 2: In a food processor, process shredded coconut until it achieved a butter-like consistency.

Step 3: Separate juice from crushed pineapple into a small bowl. Set aside.

Step 4: In a bowl of stand mixer, fitted with the paddle attachment, beat butter on medium speed, for 3-4 minutes until it becomes soft and light.

Add coconut "butter" and beat on medium speed until all is incorporated.

Step 5: Gradually add one half of powdered sugar and beat starting on low speed and continuing on medium speed until fully incorporated. Add key lime juice and beat again for 30 seconds.

Step 6: Add crushed, drained pineapples and pineapple juice. Beat until all is incorporated.

Step 7: Add remaining powdered sugar and process buttercream until smooth.

Place into the fridge to cool.

Store Pineapple Coconut Buttercream in the refrigerator for up to one week. Beat it with a mixer before using.

Caramel Buttercream

INGREDIENTS:

1/3 cup **Butter**, unsalted, softened

2 ½ cups **Sugar**, cane, powdered

1 cup **Sugar**, brown

¼ cup **Cream,** heavy

1 teaspoon **Vanilla**, pure, extract

EQUIPMENT:

Stand or hand mixer fitted with the paddle attachment, Medium saucepan, Cake decorating piping tips and bags (optional).

PREPARATION:

Step 1: Melt butter over medium heat in a medium saucepan. Add brown sugar and bring it to boil. Reduce heat to low and simmer for another 2 minutes, stirring.

Add heavy cream and bring it to boil again, stirring. Remove from heat and set aside to cool. Add vanilla and mix until it is incorporated.

Step 2: Transfer the mixture into a bowl of stand

mixer, fitted with the paddle attachment. Add powdered sugar and beat until mixture becomes soft and smooth. Do not overbeat.

Store Caramel Buttercream in the refrigerator for up to one week. Beat it with a mixer before using.

Chocolate Buttercream

INGREDIENTS:

8 Oz **Butter**, unsalted, softened

2 cups **Sugar**, powdered, sifted

½ cup **Cocoa powder,** Dutch, processed

2 tablespoons **Milk**

1 teaspoon **Vanilla**, pure, extract

EQUIPMENT:

Stand or hand mixer fitted with the paddle attachment, Sifter, Food scale or measuring cups set, Cake decorating piping tips and bags (optional).

PREPARATION:

Step 1: Place butter on a kitchen countertop and leave it until it reaches room temperature.

Step 2: In a bowl of stand mixer, fitted with the paddle attachment, beat butter on medium speed, for 3-4 minutes until it becomes soft and light.

Step 3: Gradually add one half of powdered sugar and beat starting on low speed and continuing on medium speed until fully incorporated.

Add vanilla extract and cocoa powder. Beat again for 30 seconds.

Slowly add remaining sugar and beat on medium speed until all is fully incorporated and buttercream becomes fluffy.

Place into the fridge to cool.

Store Chocolate Buttercream in the refrigerator for up to one week. Beat it with a mixer before using.

Cherry Buttercream

INGREDIENTS:

FOR THE BUTTERCREAM:

8 Oz **Butter**, unsalted, softened

2 cups **Sugar**, powdered, sifted

2 teaspoons **Vanilla**, pure, extract

FOR THE CHERRIES PUREE:

1 cup **Cherries**, frozen, thawed

2 tablespoons **Cream**, heavy, whipping

EQUIPMENT:

Stand or hand mixer fitted with the paddle attachment, Sifter, Food scale or measuring cups set, Cake decorating piping tips and bags (optional).

PREPARATION

MAKE THE PUREE:

Step 1: In a blender, puree cherries and heavy cream until smooth.

Transfer into a small saucepan, add two tablespoons of powdered sugar and reduce the liquid by simmering over low heat. Set aside to cool.

MAKE THE BUTTERCREAM:

Step 1: Place butter and frozen cherries on a kitchen countertop and leave it until it reaches room temperature.

Step 2: In a bowl of stand mixer, fitted with the paddle attachment, beat softened butter on medium speed, for 3-4 minutes until it becomes soft and light.

Step 3: Gradually add one half of powdered sugar and beat starting on low speed and continuing on medium speed until fully incorporated.

Add vanilla extract. Beat again for 30 seconds.

Slowly add remaining sugar and beat on medium speed until all is fully incorporated and buttercream becomes light and fluffy.

Step 4: Add cherry jelly and beat until all is incorporated.

Place into the fridge to cool.

Store Cherry Buttercream in the refrigerator for up to 1 week. Beat it with a mixer before using.

White Russian Buttercream

INGREDIENTS:

8 Oz **Butter**, unsalted, softened

2 cups **Sugar**, powdered, sifted

4 tablespoons **Kahlua,** liquor

2 tablespoons **Vodka**

2 teaspoons **Vanilla**, pure, extract

EQUIPMENT:

Stand or hand mixer fitted with the paddle attachment, Sifter, Food scale or measuring cups set, Cake decorating piping tips and bags (optional).

PREPARATION:

Step 1: Place butter on a kitchen countertop and leave it until it reaches room temperature.

Step 2: In a bowl of stand mixer, fitted with the paddle attachment, beat butter on medium speed, for 3-4 minutes until it becomes soft and light.

Step 3: Gradually add one half of powdered sugar and beat starting on low speed and continuing on medium speed until fully incorporated.

Add vanilla extract, vodka, and Kahlua liquor. Beat again for 30 seconds.

Slowly add remaining sugar and beat on medium speed until all is incorporated and buttercream becomes light and fluffy.

Place into the fridge to cool.

Store White Russian Buttercream in the refrigerator for up to one week. Beat it with a mixer before using.

Recipes: Cakes

Chocolate Cake Prague

INGREDIENTS:

FOR THE CAKE:

2 Cups **Flour**, white, all-purpose

1 Cup **Sugar**

6 **Eggs**

14 Oz **Condensed Milk**, sweetened

1 Cup **Buttermilk** (or sour cream), room temperature

1 Cup **Cocoa powder**, unsweetened

1 teaspoon **Baking powder**

3/4 teaspoon **Baking soda**

1/2 teaspoon **Lemon**, juice of

1/4 teaspoon **Salt,** sea salt

1/3 Cup **Vegetable oil,** olive, virgin

1 teaspoon **Vanilla,** extract, pure

Cooking spray for greasing the pans

FOR THE FROSTING:

12 Oz **Butter**, unsalted, softened

2 Cups **Sugar**, powdered

14 Oz **Condensed Milk**, sweetened

1/2 Cup **Cocoa powder**, unsweetened

1 teaspoon **Vanilla,** extract, pure

1 teaspoon **Rum** (optional)

EQUIPMENT:

Measuring cups, Two (9-inch-round, 2-inch-deep) cake pans or one (9- by 13-inch) baking pan, Stand or hand mixer fitted with the paddle attachment, Large mixing bowl, 1 to 2 wire cooling racks, Spatula or cake scraper, Cake decorating piping tips and bags (optional), Rotating cake table (optional), Parchment paper (optional).

PREPARATION:

MAKE THE CAKE:

Step 1: Preheat the oven to 355°F.

Grease the bottom and sides of two (9-inch-round, 2-inch-deep) cake pans with a cooking spray.

You can also line the bottoms of the trays with parchment paper and lightly grease the paper with the cooking spray.

Step 2: Sift and combine flour, cocoa powder, baking powder, baking soda, and salt in a large bowl.

Step 3: In a bowl of stand mixer fitted with the paddle attachment (you can use a bowl and a hand mixer) combine sugar and eggs.

Beat on low to medium speed until everything is well incorporated and achieves a smooth consistency.

Add buttermilk (or sour cream) and continue mixing until all is well incorporated.

Add vegetable oil, vanilla extract, and lemon juice. Continue mixing for another 2-3 minutes.

Step 4: Separate dry flour mix on 3 or 4 parts and add it to the wet mixture in 3 or 4 batches. Beat at low speed to incorporate.

Once all is incorporated, beat on medium speed for another 1-2 minutes. If you see the mixture is too dry, add more buttermilk or milk (little at a time).

Step 5: Separate the batter into two equal parts and spread between the two greased pans. Bake until firm for about 25 - 30 minutes or until wooden skewer tester comes out clean.

Step 6: Transfer crusts onto the cooling racks and peel off the parchment paper (if you are using it). Let the cake cool completely.

MAKE THE FROSTING:

Step 1: In a bowl of stand mixer fitted with the paddle attachment (you can use a bowl and a hand mixer) combine butter and powdered sugar.

Beat on medium speed for 2 to 3 minutes until it is fully incorporated and becomes fluffy and light in color.

Add vanilla extract and beat for another 1-2 minutes.

If you would like to decorate your cake set aside and refrigerate 1/3 of the frosting for about an hour until it becomes firm.

Step 2: Little at a time add condensed milk and beat on medium speed for to 3-5 minutes until it is fully incorporated.

ASSEMBLE THE CAKE:

If you decorate your cake set aside and refrigerate 1/3 of the frosting for about an hour until it becomes firm.

This will be your cooled frosting. The rest of the frosting will be room temperature frosting.

Step 1: If you set aside 1/3 of the frosting for cake decorating, divide the rest of the room temperature frosting into three equal parts.

(If not, divide the entire amount of yielded frosting into three equal parts).

Place a small portion (1-2 tablespoons) of frosting on top of the serving plate.

Step 2: Place the first cake layer on the serving plate and cover top of the crust with 1/3 of room temperature frosting.

Step 3: Place the second layer on top and cover it with 1/3 of room temperature frosting.

Step 4: Use the remaining 1/3 of room temperature frosting to spread on sides of the cake. Level the edges and surface of the cake with a spatula or a scraper. Place it into the fridge to cool.

Use cooled frosting to decorate the cooled cake using piping tips and bags. (Optional).

DECORATE THE CAKE:

Once you are ready to decorate your cake using piping tips and bags, remove the cooled frosting from the fridge.

Place the cooled frosting into a piping bag and start piping borders and flowers. You can also add food coloring. *(We recommend using natural food coloring instead of artificial colors).*

Store Chocolate Cake Prague in the refrigerator for up to 5 days or in the fridge for up to one month.

Black Forest Meringue Chocolate Cake

INGREDIENTS:

FOR THE CAKE:

2 Cups **Flour**, white, all-purpose

1 ½ Cups **Sugar,** white, granulated

1 Cup **Sugar**, brown

4 **Eggs**

1 Cup **Buttermilk** (or sour cream), room temperature

1 Cup **Cocoa powder**, Dutch, unsweetened

½ Cup **Chocolate,** baking, dark

1 teaspoon **Baking powder**

¾ teaspoon **Baking soda**

½ teaspoon **Lemon**, juice of

¼ teaspoon **Salt,** sea salt

¾ Cup **Vegetable oil,** olive, virgin

1 teaspoon **Vanilla,** extract, pure

Cooking spray for greasing the pans

FOR THE MERINGUE:

4 **Egg,** whites, room temperature

1 Cup **Sugar,** white, cane, granulated

1/3 teaspoon **Cream of tartar**

1 teaspoon **Vanilla**, extract, pure

FOR THE FILLING:

24 Oz **Sour cherries,** pitted (or **Tart** cherries), pitted

1 Cup **Sugar,** white, refined

¼ Cup **Cornstarch**, organic

½ Tablespoon **Vanilla,** extract, pure

FOR THE FROSTING:

2 ½ Cups **Heavy whipping cream**

3 Cups **Sugar**, powdered

1 Tablespoon **Vanilla,** extract, pure

FOR THE BUTTERCREAM:

8 Oz **Butter**, unsalted, softened

4 Cups **Sugar**, powdered

1 teaspoon **Vanilla**, extract, pure

EQUIPMENT:

Measuring cups, Two (9-inch-round, 2-inch-deep) cake pans or One (9- by 13-inch) baking pan, Medium saucepan, Large and small baking trays, Stand or hand mixer fitted with the paddle attachment, Large mixing bowl, 1 to 2 wire cooling racks, Spatula or cake scraper, Cake decorating piping tips and bags (optional), Rotating cake table (optional), Parchment paper (optional).

PREPARATION:

MAKE THE MERINGUE:

Preheat the oven to 250°F.

Step 1: In a bowl of stand mixer fitted with the paddle attachment (you can use a bowl and a hand mixer) combine egg whites, cream of tartar, and vanilla. Beat on medium speed until foamy.

One spoon at a time, add sugar and beat the mixture until sugar dissolves, then add more sugar.

Repeat.

Continue beating for 7 to 10 minutes until still glossy peaks start forming.

Step 2: Take your pastry bag and set a decorating tip with a small hole. Alternatively, you can cut a small hole in the pastry piping bag.

Step 3: Transfer meringue into the piping bag. Pipe 1.5 – 2-inch diameter cookies onto a large baking tray lined with parchment paper. Space them two inches apart.

On a small baking tray lined up with a parchment paper, pipe smaller cookies (0.5 inches) for cake decorations. Space them one inch apart.

Step 4: Place the large tray with meringues into the oven and bake the meringues for 40-45 minutes or until they become firm.

Twenty minutes into baking place the small tray with meringues into the oven. Bake the meringues for remaining 20-25 minutes.

Turn off oven and leave meringues in oven for about one hour.

Step 5: Remove meringues from the oven and separate from the parchment paper. Set aside small meringues for cake decorations.

Turn large meringues into crumbs of approximately 1/4 inch in size. Set aside.

MAKE THE CAKE:

Step 1: Preheat oven to 355°F.

Grease the bottom and sides of two (9-inch-round, 2-inch-deep) cake pans with a cooking spray.

You can also line the bottoms of the trays with parchment paper and lightly grease the paper with the cooking spray.

Step 2: Sift and combine flour, cocoa powder, baking powder, baking soda, and salt in a large bowl.

Step 3: In a bowl of stand mixer fitted with the paddle attachment (you can use a bowl and a hand mixer) combine sugar, brown sugar, and eggs.

Beat on low to medium speed until everything is well incorporated and achieves a smooth consistency.

Add buttermilk (or sour cream) and continue mixing until all is well incorporated.

Add vegetable oil, pure vanilla extract, and lemon juice. Continue mixing for another 2-3 minutes.

Step 4: Separate dry flour mix on 3 or 4 parts and add it to the wet mixture in 3 or 4 batches while beating at low speed to incorporate.

Once all is incorporated, beat on medium speed for another 1-2 minutes. If you see the mixture is too dry, add more buttermilk or milk (little at a time).

Step 5: Separate batter into two parts and spread evenly between two greased bowls. Bake until firm for about 25 - 30 minutes or until wooden skewer tester comes clean.

Step 6: Transfer the crusts onto the cooling racks and peel off the parchment paper (if you are using it). Let the cake cool completely.

MAKE THE FILLING:

Step 1: Drain the cherries, reserve and set aside the cherry juice.

In a medium-size saucepan add drained tart cherries, sugar, cornstarch, 1/2 cup of the reserved cherry juice, and vanilla extract. Whisk all together.

Step 2: Cook over low heat constantly stirring for about 10 minutes or until the mixture thickens. Set aside to cool.

MAKE THE FROSTING:

Step 1: In a bowl of stand mixer fitted with the paddle attachment (you can use a bowl and a hand mixer) combine heavy whipping cream, powdered sugar, and vanilla extract. Beat on medium speed until it becomes light and fluffy.

MAKE THE BUTTERCREAM:

Step 1: In a bowl of stand mixer fitted with the paddle attachment (you can use a bowl and a hand mixer) combine butter and powdered sugar.

Beat on medium speed for 2 to 3 minutes until it is fully incorporated and becomes fluffy and light in color.

Add vanilla extract and beat for another 1-2 minutes. Refrigerate for about one hour until it becomes firm.

ASSEMBLE THE CAKE:

Step 1: Place a small portion (1-2 tablespoons) of frosting on top of the serving plate.

Step 2: Cut cooled crusts with a knife or cake cutting tool into two pieces. You will have four cake layers.

Step 3: Place the first cake layer on the serving plate and cover top of the crust with 1/4 of the cherry filling. Place 1/4 of meringue crumbs on top of the cherry filling. Cover meringue crumbs with 1/4 of the frosting.

Step 4: Place the second cake layer on top and cover it with 1/4 of the cherry filling. Place 1/4 of meringue crumbs on top of the cherry filling. Cover meringue crumbs with 1/4 of the frosting.

Step 5: Place the third cake layer on top and cover it with 1/4 of the cherry filling. Place 1/4 of meringue crumbs on top of the cherry filling. Cover meringue crumbs with 1/4 of the frosting.

Step 6: Place the fourth cake layer on top and cover it with 1/4 of the cherry filling. Place 1/4 of meringue crumbs on top of the cherry filling. Cover meringue crumbs with 1/4 of the frosting. Level the edges and surface of the cake with a spatula or a scraper.

DECORATE THE CAKE:

Option 1: Decorate the top of the cake with cherries and reserved small meringue cookies.

Option 2: Use cake decorating tools to decorate the cake. You will need to prepare buttercream frosting for this option.

Once you are ready to decorate your cake using piping tips and bags, remove the cooled buttercream from the fridge.

Place cooled buttercream into a piping bag and start piping borders and flowers. You can also add food coloring. *(We recommend using natural food coloring instead of artificial colors).*

Add cherries and small meringue cookies as part of your cake decorating design.

Store Black Forest Meringue Chocolate Cake in the refrigerator for up to 5 days or in the fridge for up to one month.

Very Berries Chocolate Cake

INGREDIENTS:

FOR THE CAKE:

2 Cups **Flour**, all-purpose

1 ½ Cups **Sugar,** white, cane, granulated

1 Cup **Sugar**, brown

4 **Eggs**

1 Cup **Buttermilk** (or sour cream), room temperature

1 Cup **Cocoa powder**, unsweetened

½ Cup **Blueberries**, dried

½ Cup **Cranberries**, dried

½ Cup **Cherries**, dried

¼ Cup **Raspberries**, dried

1 teaspoon **Baking powder**

¾ teaspoon **Baking soda**

½ teaspoon **Lemon,** juice

¼ teaspoon **Salt**

¾ Cup **Vegetable oil,** virgin

1 teaspoon **Vanilla,** extract, pure

Cooking spray for greasing the pans

FOR THE FILLING:

12 Oz **Berries,** frozen, mixed

12 Oz **Cherries,** frozen

1 Cup **Sugar,** white, cane, granulated

½ Cup **Water**

¼ Cup **Cornstarch**, organic

½ tablespoon **Vanilla,** extract, pure

FOR THE FROSTING:

2 ½ Cups **Cream,** heavy whipping

4 Cups **Sugar**, powdered

½ Cup **Cocoa powder**, unsweetened

1 tablespoon **Vanilla,** extract, pure

EQUIPMENT:

Measuring cups, Two (9-inch-round, 2-inch-deep) cake pans or 1 (9- by 13-inch) baking pan, Medium saucepan, Stand or hand mixer fitted with the paddle attachment, Large mixing bowl, 1 to 2 wire cooling racks, Spatula or cake scraper, Cake decorating piping tips and bags (optional), Rotating cake table (optional), Parchment paper (optional).

PREPARATION:

MAKE THE CAKE:

Step 1: Preheat the oven to 355°F.

Grease the bottom and sides of two (9-inch-round, 2-inch-deep) cake pans with a cooking spray.

You can also line the bottoms of the trays with parchment paper and lightly grease the paper with the cooking spray.

Step 2: Sift and combine flour, cocoa powder, baking powder, baking soda and salt in a large bowl. (Dry mix).

Step 3: In a food processor pulse all berries until finely chopped.

Add chopped berries to the dry mix.

Step 4: In a bowl of stand mixer fitted with the paddle attachment combine sugar and eggs.

Beat on low to medium speed until everything is well incorporated and achieves a smooth consistency.

Add buttermilk (or sour cream) and continue mixing until all is well incorporated.

Add vegetable oil, vanilla extract, and lemon juice. Continue mixing for another 2-3 minutes.

Step 5: Separate dry flour mix on 3 or 4 parts and add it to the wet mixture in 3 or 4 batches while beating at low speed to incorporate. Once all is incorporated, beat on medium speed for another 1-2 minutes. If you see the mixture is too dry, add more buttermilk or milk (little by little).

Step 6: Separate the batter on two parts and spread evenly between two greased bowls. Bake until firm for about 25 - 30 minutes or until wooden skewer tester comes clean.

Step 7: Transfer the crusts onto cooling racks and peel off the parchment paper if you are using it. Let the cake cool completely.

MAKE THE FILLING:

Step 1: In a medium-size saucepan, combine frozen berries, frozen cherries, sugar, cornstarch, 1/2 cup of water and vanilla extract. Whisk all together.

Step 2: Cook over low heat, stirring, for about 10 minutes or until the mixture thickens. Set aside to cool.

MAKE THE FROSTING:

Step 1: In a bowl of stand mixer fitted with the paddle attachment (you can use a bowl and a hand mixer) combine heavy whipping cream, powdered sugar, cocoa powder, and vanilla extract.

Beat on medium speed until it becomes light and fluffy.

ASSEMBLE THE CAKE:

Step 1: Place a small portion (1-2 tablespoons) of frosting on top of the serving plate.

Step 2: Cut cooled crusts onto two pieces with a knife or cake cutting tool. You will have four cake layers.

Step 3: Place the first cake layer on the serving plate and cover top of the crust with 1/4 of the berries filling. Cover the berries filling with 1/4 of the frosting.

Step 4: Place the second cake layer on the serving plate and cover top of the crust with 1/4 of the berries filling. Cover the berries filling with 1/4 of the frosting.

Step 5: Place the third cake layer on the serving plate and cover top of the crust with 1/4 of the berries filling. Cover the berries filling with 1/4 of the frosting.

Step 6: Place the fourth cake layer on the serving plate and cover top of the crust with 1/4 of the berries filling. Cover the berries filling with 1/4 of the frosting.

Level the edges and surface with a spatula or a scraper.

DECORATE THE CAKE:

Option 1: Decorate top of the cake with cherries.

Option 2: Use cake decorating tools to decorate the cake. You will need to prepare buttercream frosting for this option.

Once you are ready to decorate your cake using piping tips and bags, remove the cooled buttercream from the fridge.

The simplest way to make the buttercream for piping is to combine 8 Oz of butter with 1 cup of powdered sugar and beat it on medium speed with a paddle attachment until it becomes light and fluffy. Then let it cool in the fridge for about 1-2 hours before using.

Place cooled buttercream into a piping bag and start piping borders and flowers. You can also add food coloring. *(We recommend using natural food coloring instead of artificial colors).*

Very Berries Chocolate Cake in the refrigerator for up to 5 days or in the fridge for up to one month.

Chocolate Cake Nutella

INGREDIENTS:

FOR THE CAKE:

2 cups **Flour**, all-purpose

1 ½ cups **Sugar**

1 cup **Sugar**, brown

4 **Eggs**

1 cup **Buttermilk** (or sour cream), room temperature

1 cup **Cocoa powder**, unsweetened

½ Cup **Chocolate chips**, bakers

1 teaspoon **Baking powder**

¾ teaspoon **Baking soda**

½ teaspoon **Lemon**, juice

¼ teaspoon **Salt**

¾ Cup **Vegetable oil**

1 teaspoon **Vanilla,** extract, pure

Cooking spray for greasing the pans

FOR THE FROSTING:

8 Oz **Butter**, unsalted, softened

7 Oz **Nutella**, hazelnut spread

6 Oz **Farmer cheese**

3 Cups **Sugar**, white, cane, powdered

1 teaspoon **Vanilla,** extract, pure

EQUIPMENT:

Measuring cups, Two (9-inch-round, 2-inch-deep) cake pans or 1 (9- by 13-inch) baking pan, Stand or hand mixer fitted with the paddle attachment, Large mixing bowl, 1 to 2 wire cooling racks, Spatula or cake scraper, Cake decorating piping tips and bags (optional), Rotating cake table (optional), Parchment paper (optional).

PREPARATION:

MAKE THE CAKE:

Step 1: Preheat the oven to 355°F.

Grease the bottom and sides of two (9-inch-round, 2-inch-deep) cake pans with a cooking spray.

You can also line the bottoms of the trays with parchment paper and lightly grease the paper with the cooking spray.

Step 2: Sift and combine flour, cocoa powder, baking powder, baking soda, chocolate chips, and salt in a large bowl.

Step 3: In a bowl of stand mixer fitted with the paddle attachment combine sugar and eggs.

Beat on low to medium speed until everything is well incorporated and achieves a smooth consistency.

Add buttermilk (or sour cream) and continue mixing until all is well incorporated.

Add vegetable oil, vanilla extract, and lemon juice. Continue mixing for another 2-3 minutes.

Step 4: Separate dry flour mix on 3 or 4 parts and add it to the wet mixture in 3 or 4 batches while beating at low speed to incorporate.

Once all is incorporated, beat on medium speed for another 1-2 minutes. If you see the mixture is too dry, add more buttermilk or milk (little by little).

Step 5: Separate the batter into two parts and spread evenly between two greased bowls. Bake until firm for about 25 - 30 minutes or until wooden skewer tester comes clean.

Step 6: Transfer the crusts onto cooling racks and peel off the parchment paper if you are using it. Let the cake cool completely.

MAKE THE FROSTING:

Step 1: In a bowl of stand mixer fitted with the paddle attachment (you can use a bowl and a hand mixer) combine butter and powdered sugar.

Beat on medium speed for 2 to 3 minutes until it is fully incorporated and becomes fluffy and light in color.

Add vanilla extract and beat for another 1-2 minutes.

If you decorate your cake, using cake decorating piping tips and bags, set aside and refrigerate 1/3 of the frosting for about an hour until it becomes firm.

Step 2: Spoon by spoon, add farmers cheese and beat on medium speed for 2 to 3 minutes until it is fully incorporated and becomes light and fluffy.

Spoon by spoon, add hazelnut spread and beat on medium speed for 3 to 4 minutes until it is fully incorporated and becomes more glossy.

ASSEMBLE THE CAKE:

If you decorate your cake set aside and refrigerate 1/3 of the frosting for about an hour until it becomes firm.

This will be your cooled frosting. The rest of the frosting will be room temperature frosting.

Step 1: If you set aside 1/3 of the frosting for cake decorating, divide the rest of the room temperature frosting into three equal parts.

(If not, divide the entire amount of yielded frosting into three equal parts).

Place a small portion (1-2 tablespoons) of frosting on top of the serving plate.

Step 2: Place the first cake layer on the serving plate and cover top of the crust with 1/3 of room temperature frosting.

Step 3: Place the second layer on top cover top of the crust with 1/3 of room temperature frosting.

Step 4: Use the remaining 1/3 of room temperature frosting to spread on sides of the cake. Smooth the surface with a spatula.

Use cooled frosting to decorate the cake using piping tips and bags.

DECORATE THE CAKE:

Once you are ready to decorate your cake using piping tips and bags, remove the cooled frosting from the fridge.

Place the cooled frosting into a piping bag and start piping borders and flowers. You can also add food coloring. *(We recommend using natural food coloring instead of artificial colors).*

Store Chocolate Cake Nutella in the refrigerator for up to 5 days or in the fridge for up to one month.

Flourless Lava Cake

INGREDIENTS:

FOR THE CAKE:

1 Cup **Sugar**

6 **Eggs**

1 ½ Cup **Butter,** unsalted, softened

1 ½ Cup **Chocolate chips**, bakers

Cooking spray for greasing the pans

FOR THE FROSTING:

1 ½ Cup **Mascarpone**

6 Oz **Butter**, unsalted, softened

1 Cup **Sugar**, cane, white, powdered

1 teaspoon **Vanilla**, extract

FOR THE CARAMEL:

¾ Cup **Water**

¾ Cup **Cream**, heavy

¾ Cup **Sugar**, powdered

1 teaspoon **Gelatin**

1 teaspoon **Starch**, potato

½ teaspoon **Salt**, Himalayan, pink

EQUIPMENT:

Measuring cups, Two (9-inch-round, 2-inch-deep) cake pans or 1 (9- by 13-inch) baking pan, Stand or hand mixer fitted with the paddle attachment, Saucepan, Medium mixing bowl, 1 to 2 wire cooling racks, Cake decorating piping tips and bags (optional), Rotating cake table (optional), Parchment paper (optional).

PREPARATION:

MAKE THE CAKE:

Step 1: Preheat the oven to 355°F.

Grease the bottom and sides of two (9-inch-round, 2-inch-deep) cake pans with a cooking spray.

You can also line the bottoms of the trays with parchment paper and lightly grease the paper with the cooking spray.

Step 2: In a saucepan melt chocolate chips and butter. (You can also use a water bath to melt chocolate chips and butter).

Step 3: Separate egg whites from yolks into two different bowls. In a bowl of stand mixer fitted with the whisk attachment add egg whites with sugar, and beat until the mixture starts forming sharp peaks.

In a separate bowl beat the egg yolks with salt with a whisk attachment, until the mixture becomes smooth and white in color.

Step 4: In a separate bowl add egg yolks and salt. Beat with the whisk attachment until the mixture becomes smooth and light color.

Step 5: Transfer the mixture into the greased cake form and place into the oven for 25-30 minutes. The middle of the cake should be quite moist.

Let the cake to cool down at room temperature for 30 minutes.

Decorate with cocoa powder.

Store Flourless Lava Cake in the refrigerator for up to 5 days or in the fridge for up to one month.

Chocolate Raspberry Cheesecake

INGREDIENTS:

FOR THE CAKE:

1 ½ Cups **Flour**, all-purpose

1 Cup **Sugar**

1/2 Cup **Sugar**, brown

6 **Eggs**

1 Cup **Cocoa powder**, Dutch, unsweetened

½ Cup **Carrots**, peeled

½ Cup **Dates,** dried, pitted

½ Cup **Applesauce,** unsweetened

½ Cup **Buttermilk**

1 teaspoon **Baking powder**

¾ teaspoon **Baking soda**

¾ teaspoon **Salt**

1 Cup **Vegetable oil,** such as unrefined olive oil

Cooking spray for greasing the springform pan

FOR THE SYRUP:

½ Cup **Raspberry preserve**, seedless

6 tablespoons **Water**

FOR THE CHEESE:

8 Oz **Cream cheese**

1 **Egg**

¼ Cup **Buttermilk**

¼ Cup **Sour cream**

1 tablespoon **Flour,** all purpose

FOR THE FROSTING:

6 Oz **Farmer cheese**

6 Oz **Butter**, unsalted, softened

2 ½ Cups **Sugar**, powdered

½ tablespoon **Vanilla,** extract

FOR THE DECORATIONS:

1 Cup **Coconut**, unsweetened, shredded

EQUIPMENT:

Measuring cups, One 9-inch springform baking pan, Small saucepan, Stand or hand mixer fitted with the paddle attachment, Small, medium and large mixing bowls, Food processor or hand grater, Spatula or cake scraper, Cake decorating piping tips and bags (optional), Rotating cake table (optional), Parchment paper (optional).

PREPARATION

MAKE THE CAKE:

Step 1: Place dates into a small bowl, cover with water. Set aside for one hour.

Step 2: Preheat the oven to 355°F.

Grease the bottom and sides of 9-inch springform pan with a cooking spray.

Step 3: In a large bowl combine flour, cocoa powder, baking powder, baking soda and salt.

Step 4: In a bowl of stand mixer fitted with the paddle attachment (you can use a bowl and a hand mixer) combine sugar and eggs.

Mix on low speed until everything is well incorporated and achieves a smooth consistency.

Add vegetable oil, buttermilk, vanilla, and applesauce. Continue mixing until all is well incorporated.

Step 5: Separate flour mix onto 3 or 4 parts and add it in 3 or 4 batches, using a spatula to fold the mixture together until all is incorporated. Fold in carrots mixing with a spatula. Set aside.

MAKE THE SYRUP:

In a small saucepan combine raspberry preserves and water. Warm up on low heat, mixing with a spatula, until melted.

MAKE THE CHEESE:

Combine cream cheese, buttermilk, sour cream, and flour. Beat the mixture with a paddle attachment until all is evenly incorporated and mixture becomes smooth.

Fold in raspberry syrup and gently mix with a spatula. Do not over mix. Let the raspberry syrup stay in small clusters.

ASSEMBLE THE CAKE:

Step 1: Pour 1/3 of cake batter into greased springform pan.

Pour 1/3 of raspberry cheese over the cake batter.

Step 2: Repeat until you place all batter and raspberry cheese into the springform pan.

BAKE THE CAKE:

Preheat the oven to 355F.

Bake the cake for about 60-65 minutes or until the center is set and not very wobbly. At 30-35 minutes into baking, cover the springform with aluminum foil to prevent burning of the top.

Once ready set it aside for an hour to cool. (Preferably leave it overnight in the fridge once it is cool).

MAKE THE FROSTING:

Step 1: In a bowl of stand mixer fitted with the

paddle attachment (you can use a bowl and a hand mixer) combine butter and powdered sugar.

Beat on medium speed for 2 to 3 minutes until it is fully incorporated and becomes fluffy and light in color.

Step 2: Spoon by spoon, add farmers cheese and beat on medium speed for 2 to 3 minutes until it is fully incorporated and becomes light and fluffy.

Add vanilla extract and beat for another 2-3 minutes.

If you decorate your cake, using cake decorating piping tips and bags, set aside and refrigerate 1/3 of the frosting for about an hour until it becomes firm.

Spread the room temperature frosting over your cake. Level the edges and surface with a spatula or scraper.

Use cooled frosting to decorate the cake using piping tips and bags.

DECORATE THE CAKE:

Cover top of cheesecake with frosting. Sprinkle with shredded coconut.

Once you are ready to decorate your cake using piping tips and bags, remove the cooled frosting from the fridge.

Place the cooled frosting into a piping bag and start piping borders and flowers. You can also add food coloring. *(We recommend using natural food coloring instead of artificial colors)*.

Store Chocolate Raspberry Cheesecake in the refrigerator for up to 5 days or in the fridge for up to one month.

Carrot Cake with Raisins

INGREDIENTS:

FOR THE CAKE:

1 lbs. **Carrots**, raw, peeled

4 **Eggs**

2 Cups **Flour**, all-purpose

2 Cups **Sugar,** cane, granulated

1 teaspoon **Baking Powder**

¾ teaspoon **Baking Soda**

¾ teaspoon **Salt,** sea, fine

1 Cup **Olive Oil,** cold pressed, virgin

½ Cup **Raisins**, golden

1 teaspoons **Cinnamon**, ground

Cooking Spray for greasing the pans

FOR THE FROSTING:

2 Cups **Sour Cream**

8 Oz **Cream Cheese**

3 Cups **Sugar**, cane, powdered

1 tablespoon **Vanilla,** pure, extract

EQUIPMENT:

Measuring cups, Two (9-inch-round, 2-inch-deep) cake pans or one (9- by 13-inch) baking pan, Medium and large mixing bowls, Stand or hand mixer fitted with the paddle attachment, One or two wire cooling racks, Food processor equipped with S-blade or hand grater, Cake decorating piping tips and bags (optional), Rotating cake table (optional), Parchment paper (optional).

PREPARATION:

MAKE THE CAKE:

Step 1: Preheat the oven to 355°F.

Grease the bottom and sides of two (9-inch-round, 2-inch-deep) cake pans with a cooking spray.

You can also line the bottoms of the trays with parchment paper and lightly grease the paper with the cooking spray.

Step 2: Grate the carrots in a food processor (or with a hand grater.

In a medium bowl, combine carrots and raisins.

Step 3: In a large bowl, combine flour, baking powder, baking soda, salt, and cinnamon.

Step 4: In a bowl of stand mixer fitted with the paddle attachment (you can use a bowl and a hand mixer) combine sugar and eggs.

Mix on low speed until everything is well incorporated and achieves a smooth consistency.

Add vegetable oil and continue mixing until all is well incorporated.

Step 5: Separate flour mix on 3 or 4 parts and add in 3 or 4 batches, using a spatula to fold the mixture together until all is incorporated. Fold in carrots and raisins.

Step 6: Separate the batter on two parts and spread evenly between two greased bowls. Bake until firm for about 25 - 30 minutes or until wooden skewer tester comes clean.

Step 7: Transfer the crusts onto cooling racks and peel off the parchment paper if you are using it. Let the cake cool completely.

MAKE THE FROSTING:

Step 1: In a bowl of stand mixer fitted with the paddle attachment combine sour cream and powdered sugar.

Beat on medium speed for 2 to 3 minutes until it is fully incorporated and becomes fluffy.

Step 2: Spoon by spoon, add cream cheese and beat on medium speed for 2 to 3 minutes until it is fully incorporated and becomes light and fluffy.

Add vanilla extract and beat for another 2-3 minutes.

This cream will not work for piping because it is too soft.

ASSEMBLE THE CAKE:

If you decorate your cake set aside and refrigerate 1/3 of the frosting for about an hour until it becomes firm.

This will be your cooled frosting. The rest of the frosting will be room temperature frosting.

Step 1: If you set aside 1/3 of the frosting for cake decorating, divide the rest of the room temperature frosting into three equal parts.

(If not, divide the entire amount of yielded frosting into three equal parts).

Place a small portion (1-2 tablespoons) of frosting on top of the serving plate.

Step 2: Place the first cake layer on the serving plate and cover top of the crust with 1/4 of the apricot jam. Place 1/3 of the room temperature frosting on top of the jam layer.

Step 3: Place the second layer on top and cover top of the crust with 1/4 of the apricot jam. Place 1/3 of the room temperature frosting on top of the jam layer.

Step 4: Use the remaining 1/3 of room temperature frosting to spread on sides of the cake. Smooth the surface with a spatula.

Use cooled frosting to decorate the cake using piping tips and bags.

DECORATE THE CAKE:

Once you are ready to decorate your cake using piping tips and bags, remove the cooled frosting from the fridge.

Place the cooled frosting into a piping bag and start piping borders and flowers. You can also add food coloring. *(We recommend using natural food coloring instead of artificial colors).*

Store Carrot Cake with Raisins in the refrigerator for up to 5 days or in the fridge for up to one month.

Pistachio Carrot Paradise Cake

INGREDIENTS:

FOR THE CAKE:

1 lbs. **Carrots**, raw, peeled

4 **Eggs**

2 Cups **Flour**, all-purpose

2 Cups **Sugar,** cane, granulated

1 teaspoon **Baking Powder**

¾ teaspoon **Baking Soda**

¾ teaspoon **Salt,** sea, fine

1 Cup **Olive Oil,** cold pressed, virgin

1/2 lbs. **Pistachios,** raw, chopped

Cooking spray for greasing the pans

FOR THE FROSTING:

½ Lbs. **Pistachio,** paste*

8 Oz **Butter**, unsalted, softened

4 Oz **Farmer Cheese**

3 Cups **Sugar**, cane, powdered

1 teaspoon **Vanilla,** extract, pure

*FOR THE PISTACHIO PASTE

½ Lbs. **Pistachios,** raw

1 ½ Cups of **Water**

½ **Lemon,** juice of

EQUIPMENT:

Measuring cups, Two (9-inch-round, 2-inch-deep) cake pans or one (9- by 13-inch) baking pan, Food processor equipped with S-blade or hand grater, Stand or hand mixer fitted with the paddle attachment, Medium and large mixing bowls, One or two wire cooling racks, Cake decorating piping tips and bags (optional), Rotating cake table (optional), Parchment paper (optional).

PREPARATION:

MAKE THE CAKE:

Step 1: Preheat the oven to 355°F.

Grease the bottom and sides of two (9-inch-round, 2-inch-deep) cake pans with a cooking spray.

You can also line the bottoms of the trays with parchment paper and lightly grease the paper with the cooking spray.

Step 2: Grate the carrots in a food processor (or with a hand grater). Pulse pistachios in a food processor (or grate with a hand grater).

In a medium mixing bowl, combine carrots and pistachios.

Step 3: In a large bowl, combine flour, baking powder, baking soda, and salt.

Step 4: In a bowl of stand mixer fitted with the paddle attachment combine sugar and eggs.

Mix on low speed until everything is well incorporated and achieves a smooth consistency.

Add vegetable oil and continue mixing until all is well incorporated.

Step 5: Separate flour mix on 3 or 4 parts and add in 3 or 4 batches, using a spatula to fold the mixture together until all is incorporated. Fold in carrots and pistachios.

Step 6: Separate the batter on two parts and spread evenly between two greased bowls. Bake until firm for about 25 - 30 minutes or until wooden skewer tester comes clean.

Step 7: Transfer the crusts onto cooling racks and peel off the parchment paper if you are using it. Let the cake cool completely.

MAKE THE PISTACHIO PASTE:

In a food processor, combine pistachios with lemon juice and start processing. If the mixture becomes dry, little by little add water until the mixture becomes a smooth and thick paste. Set aside.

MAKE THE FROSTING:

Step 1: In a bowl of stand mixer fitted with the paddle attachment combine butter and powdered sugar.

Beat on medium speed for 2 to 3 minutes until it is fully incorporated and becomes fluffy and light in color.

Step 2: Spoon by spoon, add pistachio paste and beat on medium speed for 2 to 3 minutes until it is fully incorporated. Set aside and refrigerate 1/4 of the buttercream for piping cake decorations.

Step 3: Spoon by spoon, add farmer cheese to the remaining frosting and beat on medium until it is fully incorporated.

Add vanilla extract and beat for another 2-3 minutes.

ASSEMBLE THE CAKE:

If you decorate your cake set aside and refrigerate 1/3 of the frosting for about an hour until it becomes firm.

This will be your cooled frosting. The rest of the frosting will be room temperature frosting.

Step 1: If you set aside 1/3 of the frosting for cake decorating, divide the rest of the room temperature frosting into three equal parts.

(If not, divide the entire amount of yielded frosting into three equal parts).

Place a small portion (1-2 tablespoons) of frosting on top of the serving plate.

Step 2: Place the first cake layer on the serving plate and cover top of the crust with 1/3 of room temperature frosting. Spread evenly.

Step 3: Place the second cake layer on top and cover it with 1/3 of room temperature frosting. Spread evenly.

Step 4: Use the remaining 1/3 of room temperature frosting to spread on sides of the cake. Smooth the surface with a spatula.

Use cooled frosting to decorate the cake using piping tips and bags.

DECORATE THE CAKE:

Once you are ready to decorate your cake using piping tips and bags, remove the cooled frosting from the fridge.

Place the cooled frosting into a piping bag and start piping borders and flowers. You can also add food coloring. *(We recommend using natural food coloring instead of artificial colors).*

Store Pistachio Carrot Paradise Cake in the refrigerator for up to 5 days or in the fridge for up to one month.

Carrot Coconut Cake

INGREDIENTS:

FOR THE CAKE:

1 lbs. **Carrots**, raw, peeled

4 **Eggs**

2 Cups **Flour**, all-purpose

1 Cup **Sugar,** cane, granulated

1 Cup **Sugar**, brown

1 teaspoon **Baking Powder**

¾ teaspoon **Baking Soda**

¾ teaspoon **Salt,** sea, fine

1 Cup **Olive Oil,** cold pressed, virgin

½ Cup **Macadamia Nuts,** raw, chopped

1 Cup **Coconut**, shredded, unsweetened

½ Cup **Pineapple,** dried, diced

½ Cup **Raisins**, golden

½ Cup **Apricots**, dried, diced

Cooking spray for greasing the pans

*FOR THE COCONUT PASTE:

1 Cup **Coconut**, shredded, unsweetened

1 ½ Cups of **Water**

½ **Lemon**, juice of

FOR THE FROSTING:

1 Cup **Coconut paste***

8 Oz **Cream Cheese**

8 Oz **Butter**, unsalted, softened

3 Cups **Sugar**, cane, powdered

1 tablespoon **Vanilla,** pure, extract

EQUIPMENT:

Measuring cups, Two (9-inch-round, 2-inch-deep) cake pans or 1 (9- by 13-inch) baking pan; stand or hand mixer fitted with the paddle attachment; Small, medium and large mixing bowls, 1 to 2 wire cooling racks. Food processor or hand grater. Cake decorating piping tips and bags (optional), Rotating cake table (optional), Parchment paper (optional).

PREPARATION:

MAKE THE CAKE:

Step 1: Preheat the oven to 355°F.

Grease the bottom and sides of two (9-inch-round, 2-inch-deep) cake pans with a cooking spray.

You can also line the bottoms of the trays with parchment paper and lightly grease the paper with the cooking spray.

Step 2: Grate the carrots and macadamia nuts in a food processor (or with a hand grater).

In a medium bowl, combine carrots, shredded coconut, macadamia nuts, and raisins.

Step 3: Dice dried fruits into 1/2-inch pieces. In a small bowl, combine diced pineapple and apricot. Add one cup of water and leave for about 15 minutes to soften

Step 4: In a large bowl, combine flour, baking powder, baking soda, and salt.

Step 5: In a bowl of stand mixer fitted with the paddle attachment combine sugar and eggs.

Mix on low speed until everything is well incorporated and achieves a smooth consistency.

Add vegetable oil and continue mixing until all is well incorporated.

Step 6: Separate flour mix on 3 or 4 parts and add in 3 or 4 batches, using a spatula to fold the mixture together until all is incorporated. Fold in carrots, shredded coconut, macadamia nuts, and raisins.

Drain water from the apricots and pineapples. Dry with a paper towel. Fold in apricots and pineapples.

Step 7: Separate the batter on two parts and spread evenly between two greased bowls. Bake until firm for about 25 - 30 minutes or until wooden skewer tester comes clean.

Step 8: Transfer the crusts onto cooling racks and peel off the parchment paper if you are using it. Let the cake cool completely.

MAKE THE COCONUT PASTE:

In a food processor, combine pistachios with lemon juice and start processing. If the mixture becomes dry, little by little add water until the mixture becomes smooth and thick. Set aside.

MAKE THE FROSTING:

Step 1: In a bowl of stand mixer fitted with the paddle attachment combine butter and powdered sugar.

Beat on medium speed for 2 to 3 minutes until it is fully incorporated and becomes fluffy and light in color.

Step 2: Spoon by spoon, add cream cheese and coconut paste. Beat on medium speed for 2 to 3 minutes until it is fully incorporated and becomes light and fluffy.

Add vanilla extract and beat for another 2-3 minutes.

If you decorate your cake, using cake decorating piping tips and bags, set aside and refrigerate 1/3 of the frosting for about an hour until it becomes firm.

ASSEMBLE THE CAKE:

If you decorate your cake set aside and refrigerate 1/3 of the frosting for about an hour until it becomes firm.

This will be your cooled frosting. The rest of the frosting will be room temperature frosting.

Step 1: If you set aside 1/3 of the frosting for cake decorating, divide the rest of the room temperature frosting into three equal parts.

(If not, divide the entire amount of yielded frosting into three equal parts).

Place a small portion (1-2 tablespoons) of frosting on top of the serving plate.

Step 2: Place the first cake layer on the serving plate and cover top of the crust with 1/3 of the room temperature frosting.

Step 3: Place the second cake layer on the serving plate and cover top of the crust with 1/3 of the room temperature frosting.

Step 4: Use the remaining 1/3 of room temperature frosting to spread on sides of the cake. Smooth the surface with a spatula.

Use cooled frosting to decorate the cake using piping tips and bags.

DECORATE THE CAKE:

Once you are ready to decorate your cake using piping tips and bags, remove the cooled frosting from the fridge.

Place the cooled frosting into a piping bag and start piping borders and flowers. You can also add food coloring. *(We recommend using natural food coloring instead of artificial colors).*

Store Carrot Coconut Cake in the refrigerator for up to 5 days or in the fridge for up to one month.

Carrot Sweet Potato Cheesecake

INGREDIENTS:

FOR THE CAKE:

1 lbs. **Carrots**, raw, peeled

3 **Eggs**

1 ½ Cups **Flour**, all-purpose

1 Cup **Sugar,** cane, granulated

½ Cup **Sugar**, brown

1 teaspoon **Baking Powder**

¾ teaspoon **Baking Soda**

¾ teaspoon **Salt,** sea, fine

1 Cup **Olive Oil,** cold pressed, virgin

1 Cup **Sweet Potato**, mashed

½ Cup **Applesauce,** unsweetened

½ Cup **Sour Cream**

Cooking spray for greasing the springform pan

FOR THE CHEESE:

8 Oz **Cream cheese**

1 **Egg**

½ Cup **Sour Cream**

¼ Cup **Cranberry Sauce,** canned

1 tablespoon **Flour,** all purpose

FOR THE FROSTING:

6 Oz **Farmer Cheese**

6 Oz **Butter**, unsalted, softened

2 ½ Cups **Sugar**, powdered

½ tablespoon **Vanilla,** extract

FOR THE DECORATIONS:

1 cup **Cranberries,** dried

EQUIPMENT:

Measuring cups, One 9-inch springform baking pan, Stand or hand mixer fitted with the paddle attachment, Medium and large mixing bowls, Food processor equipped with S-blade or hand grater, Cake decorating piping tips and bags (optional), Rotating cake table (optional), Parchment paper (optional).

PREPARATION:

MAKE THE CAKE:

Step 1: Preheat the oven to 355°F.

Grease the bottom and sides 9-inch springform pan with a cooking spray.

You can also line the bottom of the tray with parchment paper and lightly grease the paper with the cooking spray.

Step 2: Grate the carrots in a food processor (or with a hand grater).

Step 3: In a large bowl, combine flour, baking powder, baking soda, and salt.

Step 4: In a bowl of stand mixer fitted with the paddle attachment combine sugar and eggs.

Mix on low speed until everything is well incorporated and achieves a smooth consistency.

Add vegetable oil, buttermilk, vanilla and mashed sweet potato (puree) and applesauce. Continue mixing until all is well incorporated.

Step 5: Separate flour mix on 3 or 4 parts and add in 3 or 4 batches, using a spatula to fold the mixture together until all is incorporated. Fold in carrots mixing with a spatula. Set aside.

MAKE THE CHEESE:

Combine cream cheese, buttermilk, sour cream, and flour. Beat the mixture with a paddle attachment until all is evenly incorporated and mixture becomes smooth.

Fold in cranberry sauce and mix with a spatula.

ASSEMBLE THE CAKE:

Pour 1/3 of carrot cake batter into greased springform pan.

Pour 1/3 of cheese over the carrot batter.

Repeat until you all batter and cheese is in the springform pan.

You can swirl it with a wooden skewer to create a "marbled" effect.

BAKE THE CAKE:

Preheat the oven to 355F.

Bake the cake for about 60-65 minutes or until the center is set and not very wobbly.

At 30-35 minutes into baking, cover the springform with aluminum foil to prevent burning of the top of the cake.

Once ready set it aside for an hour to cool. (Preferably leave it overnight in the fridge once it is cool).

MAKE THE FROSTING:

Step 1: In a bowl of stand mixer fitted with the paddle attachment combine butter and powdered sugar.

Beat on medium speed for 2 to 3 minutes until it is fully incorporated and becomes fluffy and light in color.

Step 2: Spoon by spoon, add farmers cheese and beat on medium speed for 2 to 3 minutes until it is fully incorporated and becomes light and fluffy.

Add vanilla extract and beat for another 2-3 minutes.

If you decorate your cake, using cake decorating piping tips and bags, set aside and refrigerate 1/3 of the frosting for about an hour until it becomes firm.

DECORATE THE CAKE:

Cover top of cheesecake with frosting. Sprinkle with dried cranberries.

Once you are ready to decorate your cake using piping tips and bags, remove the cooled buttercream from the fridge.

Place cooled buttercream into a piping bag and start piping borders and flowers. You can also add food coloring. *(We recommend using natural food coloring instead of artificial colors).*

Store Carrot Sweet Potato Cheesecake in the refrigerator for up to 5 days or in the fridge for up to one month.

White Chocolate Raspberry Cheesecake

INGREDIENTS:

FOR THE CAKE:

2 cups **Oreo cookies,** without cream (remove)

1 ½ cups **Butter**, unsalted, softened

1/2 cup **Sugar,** white, cane, granulated

Cooking spray for greasing the springform pan

FOR THE SYRUP:

12 Oz **Raspberries**, frozen

2 cups **Sugar,** white, cane, granulated

6 tablespoons **Water**

1 tablespoon **Cornstarch**, organic

1/2 tablespoon **Vanilla,** pure, extract

FOR THE CHEESE:

32 Oz **Cream Cheese**

4 **Eggs**

1 ¼ cup **Sour Cream**

1 cup **Sugar,** white, cane, granulated

1 tablespoon **Flour,** all purpose

1/2 tablespoon **Vanilla,** pure, extract

FOR THE FROSTING:

6 Oz **Farmer Cheese**

6 Oz **Butter**, unsalted, softened

2 ½ cups **Sugar**, white, cane, powdered

1/2 tablespoon **Vanilla,** extract, pure

FOR THE DECORATIONS:

1 cup **Chocolate**, white, shaved

8 Oz **Raspberries**, fresh

EQUIPMENT:

One 9-inch springform baking pan, One larger ovenproof tray or pan to fit 9-inch springform, Aluminum foil, Small saucepan, Stand or hand mixer fitted with the paddle attachment, Large mixing bowl, Spatula or cake scraper, Cake decorating piping tips and bags (optional).

PREPARATION:

Step 1: Preheat the oven to 350°F. Line the bottom of the 9-inch springform pan with parchment paper. Grease the paper and the sides of the pan with a cooking spray.

Step 2: In a food processor, add graham cookies and process into fine crumbs. Add melted butter and sugar. Process again until all is incorporated.

Step 3: Press the cookie mix into a greased springform pan.

Step 4: Bake it for 10-15 minutes on 350°F. Set aside to cool. Reduce the oven's temperature to 325°F.

MAKE THE SYRUP:

In a small saucepan combine raspberries, sugar, and water. Let the mixture boil over medium heat, constantly stirring it. Add cornstarch and vanilla.

Once the mixture thickens, turn off the heat and set the syrup aside to cool.

MAKE THE CHEESE:

Step 1: Add all cream cheese into a bowl of stand mixer (or use a large bowl and hand mixer with paddle attachment) equipped with the paddle attachment. Beat on low to medium until cream cheese softens and becomes smooth.

Step 2: Add sour cream, eggs, vanilla extract, sugar, and flour into the bowl with cream cheese. Beat the mixture with the paddle attachment until all is evenly incorporated and mixture becomes smooth. Do not overbeat, or the cake will crack.

Step 3: Fold in raspberry syrup, gently mixing with a spatula. Do not over mix. Leave small chunks of the raspberries cluster together.

ASSEMBLE THE CAKE:

Step 1: Pour cake batter into the greased springform pan. Pour raspberry cheese over the cake batter.

Step 2: Prepare the water-bath. Cover the bottom of springform pan with aluminum foil. Place it into a larger ovenproof tray. Pour one inch of boiling water into the larger tray. (Do not let water get into the cheesecake).

BAKE THE CAKE:

Step 1: Bake the cake at 325°F for about one hour and ten minutes or until the center of the cake is set and not very wobbly. At 30-35 minutes into baking, cover the springform with aluminum foil to prevent burning of the top of the cake.

Step 2: After one hour and ten minutes turn the oven off and leave the cheesecake inside the oven (with oven door closed) for two hours.

Step 3: After two hours, set it aside to cool at room temperature. Cheesecake tastes best the next day. Once the cheesecake is cooled to a room temperature leave it overnight in the fridge.

MAKE THE FROSTING:

Step 1: Combine butter and powdered sugar in a bowl of stand mixer fitted with the paddle attachment (you can use a bowl and a hand mixer).

Beat on medium speed for 2 to 3 minutes until it is fully incorporated and becomes fluffy and light in color.

Step 2: Spoon by spoon, add farmers cheese and beat on medium speed for 2 to 3 minutes until it is fully incorporated and becomes light and fluffy.

Add vanilla extract and beat for another 2-3 minutes.

If you decorate your cake, using cake decorating piping tips and bags, set aside and refrigerate 1/3 of the frosting for about an hour until it becomes firm.

This will be your cooled frosting. The rest of the frosting will be room temperature frosting. Cover top of cheesecake with frosting. Sprinkle with shredded coconut. Decorate with fresh raspberries.

DECORATE THE CAKE:

If you are decorating your cake with cake decorating tools, once you are ready to decorate your cake, remove the cooled frosting from the fridge.

Place the cooled frosting into a piping bag and start piping borders and flowers. You can also add food coloring. *(We recommend using natural food coloring instead of artificial colors).*

White Chocolate Raspberry Cheesecake will keep for up to five days in a fridge or one month in a freezer.

Oreo Cookies Cheesecake

INGREDIENTS:

FOR THE CAKE CRUST:

2 cups **Oreo Cookies**

1 ½ cups **Butter**, unsalted, softened

1/2 cup **Sugar,** cane, granulated

Cooking spray for greasing the springform pan

FOR THE CHEESE:

24 Oz **Cream Cheese**

3 **Eggs**

1 cup **Sugar,** cane, granulated

1 cup **Sour Cream**

1 cup **Oreo Cookies,** crushed

3 tablespoon **Flour,** all purpose

1/2 teaspoon **Vanilla**, extract, pure

FOR THE FROSTING:

6 Oz **Butter**, unsalted, softened

6 Oz **Farmer Cheese**

2 ½ cups **Sugar**, cane, powdered

1 teaspoon **Vanilla**, extract, pure

EQUIPMENT:

One 9-inch springform baking pan, One larger ovenproof tray or pan to fit 9-inch springform, Aluminum foil, Stand or hand mixer fitted with the paddle attachment, Zip lock bag and Rolling pin, Food processor, Large mixing bowl, Spatula, Cake scraper, Parchment paper, Cake decorating piping tips and bags (optional).

PREPARATION:

MAKE THE CAKE:

Step 1: Preheat the oven to 350°F. Line the bottom of the 9-inch springform pan with parchment paper. Grease the paper and the sides of the pan with a cooking spray.

Step 2: In a food processor, add Oreo cookies and process into fine crumbs. Add melted butter and sugar. Process again until all is incorporated.

Step 3: Press the cookie mixture into the greased springform pan.

Step 4: Bake it for 10-15 minutes on 350°F. Set aside to cool. Reduce the oven's temperature to 325°F.

MAKE THE CHEESE:

Step 1: Place Oreo cookies into a Ziplock bag. Crush cookies with a rolling pin into small (approximately 1/4 inches) crumbs. (Alternatively, you can pulse cookies in a food processor).

Step 2: Add all cream cheese into a bowl of stand mixer (or use a large bowl and hand mixer with paddle attachment) equipped with the paddle attachment. Beat on low to medium until cream cheese softens and becomes smooth.

Step 3: Add eggs (one at a time), sugar, sour cream, vanilla extract, and flour into the bowl with cream cheese. Beat the mixture with the paddle attachment until all is evenly incorporated and mixture becomes smooth. Do not overbeat, or the cake will crack.

Fold in crushed Oreo cookies. Mix with a spatula.

ASSEMBLE THE CAKE:

Step 1: Pour cheese batter over the Oreo cookies crust.

Step 2: Prepare the water-bath. Cover the bottom of springform pan with aluminum foil. Place it into a larger ovenproof tray. Pour one inch of boiling water into the larger tray. (Do not let water get into the cheesecake).

BAKE THE CAKE:

Step 1: Bake the cake at 325°F for about one hour and ten minutes or until the center of the cake is set and not very wobbly. At 30-35 minutes into baking, cover the springform with aluminum foil to prevent burning of the top of the cake.

Step 2: After one hour and ten minutes turn the oven off and leave the cheesecake inside the oven (with oven door closed) for two hours.

Step 3: After two hours, set it aside to cool at room temperature. Cheesecake tastes best the next day. Once the cheesecake is cooled to a room temperature leave it overnight in the fridge.

MAKE THE FROSTING:

Step 1: Combine butter and powdered sugar in a bowl of stand mixer fitted with the paddle attachment (you can use a bowl and a hand mixer).

Beat on medium speed for 2 to 3 minutes until it is fully incorporated and becomes fluffy and light in color.

Step 2: Spoon by spoon, add farmers cheese and beat on medium speed for 2 to 3 minutes until it is fully incorporated and becomes light and fluffy.

Add vanilla extract and beat for another 2-3 minutes.

If you decorate your cake, using cake decorating piping tips and bags, set aside and refrigerate 1/3 of the frosting for about an hour until it becomes firm.

This will be your cooled frosting. The rest of the frosting will be room temperature frosting.

Cover the top of cheesecake with frosting. Decorate with Oreo cookies.

DECORATE THE CAKE:

If you are decorating your cake with cake decorating tools, once you are ready to decorate your cake, remove the cooled frosting from the fridge.

Place the cooled frosting into a piping bag and start piping borders and flowers. You can also add food coloring. *(We recommend using natural food coloring instead of artificial colors).*

Oreo Cookies Cheesecake will keep for up to five days in a fridge or one month in a freezer.

Recipes: Cupcakes

Basic Chocolate Cupcakes

INGREDIENTS:

FOR THE CUPCAKES:

2 Cups **Flour**, all-purpose

1 ½ Cups **Sugar**

1 Cup **Sugar**, brown

4 **Eggs**

1 Cup **Buttermilk** (or sour cream), room temperature

1 Cup **Cocoa powder**, unsweetened

1 teaspoon **Baking powder**

¾ teaspoon **Baking soda**

½ teaspoon **Lemon**, juice

¼ teaspoon **Salt**

¾ Cup **Vegetable oil**, virgin

1 teaspoon **Vanilla,** extract, pure

Cooking spray for greasing the pans

FOR THE FROSTING:

8 Oz **Butter**, unsalted, softened

4 Cups **Sugar**, powdered

1 teaspoon **Vanilla,** extract, pure

FOR THE CHOCOLATE GLAZE:

1 Cup **Chocolate**, dark, bakers

½ Cups **Sugar**, white, cane, powdered

½ Cup **Heavy Whipping Cream**

1 teaspoon **Vanilla**, pure, extract

½ teaspoon **Salt**, sea, fine

FOR THE DECORATIONS:

Chocolate coins for decorations

EQUIPMENT:

Measuring cups, Two cupcakes forms, Stand or hand mixer fitted with the paddle attachment, Large mixing bowl, 1 to 2 wire cooling racks, Spatula or cake scraper, Piping bag, Cake decorating piping tips and bags (optional), Rotating cake table (optional), Parchment paper (optional).

PREPARATION:

MAKE THE CUPCAKES:

Step 1: Preheat the oven to 355°F.

Grease the bottom and sides of two cupcakes forms with a cooking spray.

You can also line forms with cupcake liners and lightly grease the liners with the cooking spray.

Step 2: Sift and combine flour, cocoa powder, baking powder, baking soda, and salt in a large bowl.

Step 3: In a bowl of stand mixer fitted with the paddle attachment (you can use a bowl and a hand mixer) combine sugar and eggs.

Step 4: In a bowl of stand mixer fitted with the paddle attachment (you can use a bowl and a hand mixer) combine sugar and eggs.

Beat on low to medium speed until everything is well incorporated and achieves a smooth consistency.

Add buttermilk (or sour cream) and continue mixing until all is well incorporated.

Add vegetable oil, vanilla extract, and lemon juice. Continue mixing for another 2-3 minutes.

Step 5: Separate dry flour mix on 3 or 4 parts and add it to the wet mixture in 3 or 4 batches while beating at low speed to incorporate.

Once all is incorporated, beat on medium speed for another 1-2 minutes. If you see the mixture is too dry, add more buttermilk or milk (little by little).

Step 6: Place batter into a piping bag. Pipe batter into cupcakes forms. Bake until firm for about 25 - 30 minutes or until wooden skewer tester comes out clean.

Step 7: Transfer cupcakes onto the cooling racks and peel off the parchment paper (if you are using it). Let the cupcakes cool completely.

MAKE THE FROSTING:

In a bowl of stand mixer fitted with the paddle attachment (you can use a bowl and a hand mixer) combine butter and powdered sugar.

Beat on medium speed for 2 to 3 minutes until it is fully incorporated and becomes fluffy and light in color.

Add vanilla extract and beat for another 1-2 minutes.

If you decorate your cupcakes, using cake decorating piping tips and bags, set aside and refrigerate 1/3 of the frosting for about an hour until it becomes firm.

MAKE THE CHOCOLATE GLAZE:

Step 1: Place chocolate into a heatproof bowl over a water bath. Heat over low-medium heat until the chocolate melts. Remove from heat and set aside.

Step 2: Place heavy cream into a bowl of stand mixer. Beat on medium speed with the paddle attachment until cream becomes soft and fluffy.

Add chocolate, powdered sugar, salt, and vanilla extract. Beat on medium speed for 30-45 seconds to combine. Set aside.

ASSEMBLE THE CUPCAKES:

Step 1: Cut the cupcakes into two parts. You will have two layers.

Step 2: Place the first cupcakes layers on the serving plate and cover with room temperature frosting.

Step 3: Place second layers on top and cover with remaining room temperature frosting.

Step 4: Level the edges and surface with a spatula or a scraper.

Use cooled frosting to decorate the cupcakes using piping tips and bags. (Optional).

DECORATE THE CUPCAKES:

Once you are ready to decorate your cupcakes using piping tips and bags, remove the cooled frosting from the fridge.

Place the cooled frosting into a piping bag and start piping swirls and flowers. You can also add food coloring. *(We recommend using natural food coloring instead of artificial colors).*

Store Basic Chocolate Cupcakes in the refrigerator for up

to 5 days or in the fridge for up to one month.

Choco Coco Nut Cupcakes

INGREDIENTS:

FOR THE CUPCAKES:

2 Cups **Flour**, all-purpose

1 ½ Cups **Sugar,** white, cane, granulated

1 Cup **Sugar**, brown

4 **Eggs**

1 Cup **Buttermilk** (or sour cream), room temperature

1 Cup **Cocoa powder**, Dutch, unsweetened

1 Cup **Chocolate chips**, dark, bakers

1 Cup **Coconut**, shredded, unsweetened

1 teaspoon **Baking powder**

¾ teaspoon **Baking soda**

½ teaspoon **Lemon**, juice

¼ teaspoon **Salt, fine, sea**

¾ Cup **Vegetable oil,** such as virgin olive oil

1 teaspoon **Vanilla,** extract, pure

Cooking spray for greasing the pans

*FOR THE MACADAMIA NUT PASTE:

1 cup **Macadamia nuts**, roasted

3 tablespoons **Coconut oil**, unrefined

1 teaspoon **Lemon**, juice

1 cup **Water**

FOR THE FROSTING:

8 Oz **Butter**, unsalted, softened

6 Oz **Cream cheese**

1 Cup **Macadamia**, paste*

4 Cups **Sugar**, white, cane, powdered

1 teaspoon **Vanilla,** extract, pure

EQUIPMENT:

Measuring cups, Two cupcake forms, Stand or hand mixer fitted with the paddle attachment, Large mixing bowl, 1 to 2 wire cooling racks, Spatula or cake scraper, Piping bag, Cake decorating piping tips and bags (optional), Rotating cake table (optional), Parchment paper (optional).

PREPARATION:

MAKE THE CUPCAKES:

Step 1: Preheat the oven to 355°F.

Grease the bottom and sides of two cupcakes forms with a cooking spray.

You can also line forms with cupcake liners and lightly grease the liners with the cooking spray.

Step 2: Sift and combine flour, cocoa powder, baking powder, baking soda, chocolate chips, and salt in a large bowl.

Step 3: In a bowl of stand mixer fitted with the paddle attachment combine sugar and eggs.

Beat on low to medium speed until everything is well incorporated and achieves a smooth consistency.

Add buttermilk (or sour cream) and continue mixing until all is well incorporated.

Add vegetable oil, vanilla extract, and lemon juice. Continue mixing for another 2-3 minutes.

Step 4: Separate dry flour mix on 3 or 4 parts and add it to the wet mixture in 3 or 4 batches while beating at low speed to incorporate.

Once all is incorporated, beat on medium speed for another 1-2 minutes. If you see the mixture is too dry, add more buttermilk or milk (little by little).

Fold in shredded coconut and mix with a spatula.

Step 5: Place batter into a piping bag. Pipe batter into cupcakes forms. Bake until firm for about 25 - 30 minutes or until wooden skewer tester comes out clean.

Step 6: Transfer cupcakes onto the cooling racks and peel off the parchment paper (if you are using it). Let the cupcakes cool completely.

MAKE THE MACADAMIA PASTE:

In a food processor, combine macadamia nuts with lemon juice and start processing. If the mixture becomes dry, little by little, add water until the mixture becomes a smooth and thick paste. Set aside.

MAKE THE FROSTING:

Step 1: In a bowl of stand mixer fitted with the paddle attachment combine butter and powdered sugar.

Beat on medium speed for 2 to 3 minutes until it is fully incorporated and becomes fluffy and light in color.

Step 2: Spoon by spoon, add macadamia paste and beat on medium speed for 2 to 3 minutes until it is fully incorporated. Set aside and refrigerate 1/4 of the buttercream for piping cake decorations.

Step 3: Spoon by spoon, add cream cheese to the remaining 3/4 of the frosting and beat on medium until it is fully incorporated.

Add vanilla extract and beat for another 2-3 minutes.

ASSEMBLE THE CUPCAKES:

If you decorate your cupcakes set aside and refrigerate 1/2 of the frosting for about an hour until it becomes firm.

This will be your cooled frosting. The rest of the frosting will be room temperature frosting.

Step 1: If you set aside 1/2 of the frosting for decorating, divide the rest of the room temperature frosting into three equal parts.

(If not, divide the entire amount of yielded frosting into three equal parts).

Step 2: Cut each cupcake into thee parts. You will have two layers.

Step 3: Place first cupcakes layers on the serving plate and cover with 1/2 of room temperature frosting. Spread evenly.

Step 4: Place second cupcakes layers on the serving plate and cover with 1/2 of room temperature frosting. Spread evenly.

Use cooled frosting to decorate the cupcakes using piping tips and bags.

DECORATE THE CUPCAKES:

Once you are ready to decorate your cupcakes using piping tips and bags, remove the cooled frosting from the fridge.

Place the cooled frosting into a piping bag and start piping swirls and flowers. You can also add food coloring. *(We recommend using natural food coloring instead of artificial colors).*

Store Choco Coco Nut Cupcakes in the refrigerator for up to 5 days or in the fridge for up to one month.

Chocolate Lemon Cupcakes with Pistachio Buttercream

INGREDIENTS:

FOR THE CUPCAKES:

2 Cups **Flour**, all-purpose

1 ½ Cups **Sugar**

1 Cup **Sugar**, brown

4 **Eggs**

1 Cup **Buttermilk** (or sour cream), room temperature

1 Cup **Cocoa powder**, unsweetened

1 teaspoon **Baking powder**

¾ teaspoon **Baking soda**

½ teaspoon **Lemon**, juice

¼ teaspoon **Salt**

¾ Cup **Vegetable oil,** such as unrefined olive oil

1 teaspoon **Vanilla,** extract, pure

Cooking spray for greasing the pans

FOR THE FROSTING:

½ Lbs. **Pistachio,** paste*

8 Oz **Butter**, unsalted, softened

4 Oz **Farmer cheese**

3 cups **Sugar**, powdered

1 tablespoon **Lime juice**

1 teaspoon **Vanilla,** extract, pure

FOR THE PISTACHIO PASTE*

1/2 Lbs. **Pistachios**

1 ½ Cups of **Water**

½ **Lemon,** juice of

EQUIPMENT:

Measuring cups, Two cupcake forms, Stand or hand mixer fitted with the paddle attachment, Food processor, Large mixing bowl, 1 to 2 wire cooling racks, Spatula or cake scraper, Piping bag, Cake decorating piping tips and bags (optional), Rotating cake table (optional), Parchment paper (optional).

PREPARATION:

MAKE THE CUPCAKES:

Step 1: Preheat the oven to 355°F.

Grease the bottom and sides of two cupcakes forms with a cooking spray.

You can also line forms with cupcake liners and lightly grease the liners with the cooking spray.

Step 2: In a large bowl, sift and combine flour, cocoa powder, baking powder, baking soda, and salt.

Step 3: In a bowl of stand mixer fitted with the paddle attachment combine sugar and eggs.

Beat on low to medium speed until everything is well incorporated and achieves a smooth consistency.

Add buttermilk (or sour cream) and continue mixing until all is well incorporated.

Add vegetable oil, vanilla extract, and lemon juice. Continue mixing for another 2-3 minutes.

Step 4: Separate dry flour mix on 3 or 4 parts and add it to the wet mixture in 3 or 4 batches while beating at low speed to incorporate.

Once all is incorporated, beat on medium speed for another 1-2 minutes. If you see the mixture is too dry, add more buttermilk or milk (little by little).

Step 5: Place batter into a piping bag. Pipe batter into cupcakes forms. Bake until firm for about 25 - 30 minutes or until wooden skewer tester comes out clean.

Step 6: Transfer cupcakes onto the cooling racks and peel off the parchment paper (if you are using it). Let the cupcakes cool completely.

MAKE THE PISTACHIO PASTE:

In a food processor, combine pistachios with lemon juice and start processing. If the mixture becomes dry, little by little add water until the mixture becomes a smooth and thick paste. Set aside.

MAKE THE FROSTING:

Step 1: In a bowl of stand mixer fitted with the paddle attachment combine butter and powdered sugar.

Beat on medium speed for 2 to 3 minutes until it is fully incorporated and becomes fluffy and light in color.

Step 2: Spoon by spoon, add pistachio paste and beat on medium speed for 2 to 3 minutes until it is fully incorporated. Set aside and refrigerate 1/4 of the buttercream for piping cake decorations.

Step 3: Spoon by spoon, add farmer cheese to the remaining frosting and beat on medium until it is fully incorporated.

Add vanilla extract and lime juice and beat for another 2-3 minutes.

ASSEMBLE THE CUPCAKES:

If you decorate your cupcakes set aside and refrigerate 1/3 of the frosting for about an hour until it becomes firm.

This will be your cooled frosting. The rest of the frosting will be room temperature frosting.

Step 1: If you set aside 1/3 of the frosting for decorating, divide the rest of the room temperature frosting into three equal parts.

(If not, divide the entire amount of yielded frosting into three equal parts).

Step 2: Cut cupcakes into two parts each. You will have two layers.

Step 3: Place first cupcakes layers on the serving plate and cover with 1/3 of room temperature frosting.

Step 4: Place second cupcakes layers on the serving plate and cover with 1/3 of room temperature frosting.

Step 5: Use the remaining 1/3 of room temperature frosting to spread on top of the cupcakes. Level the edges and surface with a spatula or a scraper.

DECORATE THE CUPCAKES:

Once you are ready to decorate your cupcakes using piping tips and bags, remove the cooled frosting from the fridge.

Place the cooled frosting into a piping bag and start piping swirls and flowers. You can also add food coloring. *(We recommend using natural food coloring instead of artificial colors).*

Store Chocolate Lemon Cupcakes in the refrigerator for up to 5 days or in the fridge for up to one month.

Chocolate Tropicana Cupcakes

INGREDIENTS:

FOR THE CUPCAKES:

2 Cups **Flour**, all-purpose

1 ½ Cups **Sugar,** white, cane, granulated

1 Cup **Sugar**, brown

4 **Eggs**

1 Cup **Buttermilk** (or sour cream), room temperature

1 Cup **Cocoa powder**, unsweetened

1 teaspoon **Baking powder**

¾ teaspoon **Baking soda**

½ teaspoon **Lemon**, juice

¼ teaspoon **Salt**

¾ Cup **Vegetable oil**, such as virgin olive oil

½ Cup **Walnuts,** chopped

½ Cup **Pineapple,** dried, diced

½ Cup **Raisins**, dark

½ Cup **Apricots**, dried, diced

½ teaspoon **Cinnamon**, ground

1 teaspoon **Vanilla,** extract, pure

Cooking spray for greasing the pans

FOR THE FROSTING:

8 Oz **Cream cheese**

8 Oz **Farmer cheese** (optional, then use 16 **Oz Cream cheese**)

8 Oz **Butter**, unsalted, softened

5 Cups **Sugar**, white, cane, powdered

1 tablespoon **Vanilla,** extract, pure

½ Cup **Apricot jam** (optional)

EQUIPMENT:

Measuring cups, Two cupcake forms, Stand or hand

mixer fitted with the paddle attachment, Large mixing bowl, 1 to 2 wire cooling racks, Spatula or cake scraper, Piping bag, Cake decorating piping tips and bags (optional), Rotating cake table (optional), Parchment paper (optional).

PREPARATION:

MAKE THE CUPCAKES:

Step 1: Preheat the oven to 355°F.

Grease the bottom and sides of two cupcakes forms with a cooking spray.

You can also line forms with cupcake liners and lightly grease the liners with the cooking spray.

Step 2: Sift a and combine flour, cocoa powder, baking powder, baking soda, cinnamon and salt in a large bowl.

In a food processor combine dried fruit and nuts. Pulse until chopped.

Step 3: In a bowl of stand mixer fitted with the paddle attachment combine sugar and eggs.

Beat on low to medium speed until everything is well incorporated and achieves a smooth consistency.

Add buttermilk (or sour cream) and continue mixing until all is well incorporated.

Add vegetable oil, vanilla extract, and lemon juice. Continue mixing for another 2-3 minutes.

Step 4: Separate dry flour mix on 3 or 4 parts and add it to the wet mixture in 3 or 4 batches while beating at low speed to incorporate.

Once all is incorporated, beat on medium speed for another 1-2 minutes. If you see the mixture is too dry, add a more milk (little by little).

Step 5: Fold in fruit and nut mix and mix with a spatula until it fully incorporates into the batter.

Step 6: Place batter into a piping bag. Pipe batter into cupcakes forms. Bake until firm for about 25 - 30 minutes or until wooden skewer tester comes out clean.

Step 7: Transfer cupcakes onto the cooling racks and peel off the parchment paper (if you are using it). Let the cupcakes cool completely.

MAKE THE FROSTING:

Step 1: In a bowl of stand mixer fitted with the paddle attachment (you can use a bowl and a hand mixer) combine butter and powdered sugar.

Beat on medium speed for 2 to 3 minutes until it is fully incorporated and becomes fluffy and light in color.

Step 2: Spoon by spoon, add cream cheese and farmer cheese and beat on medium speed for 2 to 3 minutes until it is fully incorporated and becomes light and fluffy.

Add vanilla extract and beat for another 2-3 minutes.

If you decorate your cake, using cake decorating piping tips and bags, set aside and refrigerate 1/3 of the frosting for about an hour until it becomes firm.

ASSEMBLE THE CUPCAKES:

If you decorate your cake set aside and refrigerate 1/3 of the frosting for about an hour until it becomes firm.

This will be your cooled frosting. The rest of the frosting will be room temperature frosting.

Step 1: If you set aside 1/3 of the frosting for cake decorating, divide the rest of the room temperature frosting into three equal parts.

(If not, divide the entire amount of yielded frosting into three equal parts).

Step 2: Cut each cupcake into two parts. You will have two levels.

Step 3: Place first cupcakes layers on the serving plate and cover with 1/2 of the apricot jam. Place 1/2 of the room temperature frosting on top of the jam layers.

Step 4: Place second cupcakes layers on the serving plate and cover with 1/2 of the apricot jam. Place 1/2 of the room temperature frosting on top of the jam layers.

Use cooled frosting to decorate the cupcakes using piping tips and bags.

DECORATE THE CUPCAKES:

Once you are ready to decorate your cupcakes using piping tips and bags, remove the cooled frosting from the fridge.

Place the cooled frosting into a piping bag and start piping swirls and flowers. You can also add food coloring. *(We recommend using natural food coloring instead of artificial colors).*

Store Chocolate Tropicana Cupcakes in the refrigerator for up to 5 days or in the fridge for up to one month.

Thank You for Purchasing This Book!

I create and test recipes for you. I hope you enjoyed these recipes.

Your review of this book helps me succeed & grow. If you enjoyed this book, please leave me a short (1-2 sentence) review on Amazon.

Thank you so much for reviewing this book!

Do you have any questions?
Email me at: **Maria@BRILLIANTkithenideas.com**

MARIA SOBININA
BRILLIANT kitchen ideas

Would you like to learn cooking techniques and tips? Visit us at:

www. BRILLIANTkitchenideas.com

Printed in Germany
by Amazon Distribution
GmbH, Leipzig